Kama Sutra II Sex Position Guide

8 in 1

OVER 250+ Sex Positions | Spice up your Sexual Life and Increase your Confidence in Bed - Sex Games Guide, Tantric Sex & Dirty Talk

Lana Fox

Table of contents

INTRODUCTION 19

HOW TO FLIRT AND SEDUCE..21

Flirting 21

Basics of courtship and how to do it 22

INTIMACY: IMPORTANCE OF IT AND HOW TO PRACTICE
....24

What is Intimacy...24

Tips 25

Physical and Sexual Intimacy 27

THE BASIS OF FOREPLAY 29

Erogenous Zones...29

Bottoms of feet 30

Armpits...30

Neck 30

Behind the knee 30

Ears 31

Hands 31

Inner thighs 31

Genital region 31

Nipples 32

Scalp...32

BEST WAYS FOR FOREPLAY 33

Different Types of Kiss 33

Measured kiss...33

Throbbing kiss..33

Askew kiss..33

Bent kiss.. 33

Direct kiss... 33

Pressure kiss.. 34

Top kiss.. 34

Distraction kiss... 34

Clip kiss.. 34

Stirring kiss.. 34

Contact kiss.. 34

Kiss to ignite the flame 34

Eyelash kiss.. 35

Finger kiss 35

Reflecting kiss 35

Scratching 35

Sounding.. 35

Half Moon.. 35

Circle 35

Line.. 35

Tiger's Nail 36

Peacock's Foot.. 36

The Jump of a Hare.. 36

Leaf of a Blue Lotus... 36

Eight bites of love 36

Gudhaka.. 36

Uchhunaka 36

Bindu.. 36

Bindu Mala 37

Pravalamani 37

4

Mani Mala 37

Khandabhraka 37

Varaha Charvita 37

Sucking the mango fruit: fellatio techniques 37

Touching 38

Nominal Congress..38

Biting the Sides 38

Kissing 38

Rubbing 38

Sucking a Mango Fruit 38

Swallowing Up...38

Outer Pincers...38

Inner Pincers 38

Let your senses evolve 38

HOW TO MAKE FOREPLAY LAST LONG 39

Extending Foreplay and Slowing Sex 40

Exploring Your Partner..41

WHAT IS TANTRIC SEX 44

The True Story Of Tantra - What Is And What Is Not...................45

The Origins 46

How it arrived in the West...47

Tantra & The Meaning Of Tantric Sex 48

The 3 Golden Rules For Tantric Sex.................................51

TANTRIC SEX CONCEPTS 52

The 4 Key Principles For Sexual Ecstasy...........................53

The attention or body awareness.....................................54

Movement and rhythm 54

5

The sound 55

Breathing 55

To summarize... 56

The Orgasm In Tantric Sex 56

Pure Bliss: What Is The Valley Orgasm? 58

How To Reach The Valley Orgasm? 59

TANTRIC SEX TECHNIQUES 60

The 10 Tantric Sex Positions 60

Lotus Position 61

Lotus Variant 61

Ground Position 61

Tantric Positions With Chair 61

Crouching 61

The Bomb 62

Tantric Positions In Water 62

Tantric Position In Bathtub 62

The Tantric Massage: What Is It & How To Do It 62

How To Do The Tantric Massage 62

All The Benefits Of Tantric Massage 63

Tantra Kundalini Massage 63

MULTIPLE ORGASM 65

Male Orgasm Basics 65

Orgasm and Ejaculation 65

How to Stimulate the Prostate to Achieve Orgasm 66

Female Orgasm Basics 66

How to Stimulate the Clitoris to Achieve Orgasm 66

How to Stimulate the G-Spot to Achieve Orgasm 66

SEX GAMES 68

Role Playing Games 69

Erotic Role Playing Games: Why try them? 69

The gardener 70

The Hitchhiker 70

Back to School 71

The Servant 71

The Spy 71

Once Upon a Time 71

The Strangers 72

The Porn Movie 72

Hot Ideas To Try At Least Once In a Lifetime 72

The Mirror 72

Come Here And Now 72

Shoes Up 72

Stop-And-Go 73

Remote Vibrator 73

Double mint 73

Slow Sex 73

Open 73

The Latex 73

Briefs in the drawer 73

Ciak, Action! 73

The Sex Compilation 74

Furniture 74

The Magic Balls 74

I Finished The Laundry 74

The Route Of The Gorge 74

Look At Me! 74

Striptease Of Balloons 74

The Lubricant 74

The Film 74

At Parents' Home 75

The Vortex 75

SEX TOYS 75

Introductions 75

The History Of Sex Toys 77

Sex Toys Types For Couples 78

Vibrator 79

Hot little Animals 79

Teasing Feather 79

Hot Dice 79

The Hot Massager 80

Soft Handcuffs 80

Geisha Balls 80

Sex Toys: A Guide To Choosing The Right One 80

Sex toy: where to buy it 80

Sex toy: choose by material 81

Sex toys: choose according to price 81

Sex toys: how they work 82

Tips for use and storage 82

Sex toys: types to choose from 82

17 + 1 Sex Toys For Intense Orgasms 83

Ki-Wi 83

Nobessence 84

Zoon + ...84

Tor...84

Ina 84

Squeel 84

Lovemoiselle..85

Eve 85

Form 2 85

Better Than Chocolate...85

Pure Wand 85

Bcurious 85

Contour Q..86

Teneo Uno and Duo...86

Tickle-Popzzz...86

Kokeshi Dancer 86

Sexy Bunny 86

Cry baby 86

Sex Toys: 5 Taboos To Break..87

1 - Sex toys are not only vibrators..87

4 - Sex toys are not a substitute of the male or "natural" sex 88

5 - Sex toys are not dirty games 88

ANAL SEX 88

Anal Sex: Normal or Not? 88

An Introduction to Anal Sex..89

Take the anal training before going the whole way. 89

The lube is mandatory 89

Never leave home without a condom. 90

Foreplay is important 90

Maintain the basic hygiene 90

Anal activities 90

Anal sex 91

Prostate stimulation... 91

Pegging 91

Butt plugs 91

The Anal Sex Positions to Try 92

Sitting Dog 92

Flying Doggie 92

Doggy Angle 92

Froggie... 92

Reverse Froggie 92

Standing 93

Upright Missionary... 93

Missionary L 93

Spoon and Fork 93

The Jockey Sex.. 93

Highchair 94

Reverse Isis... 94

The Split.. 94

The Burning Man.. 94

YabYum 95

The Chairman 95

Lap Dance.. 95

Tailgate.. 95

Horizontal Tailgate 96

The Turtle Position 96

Stallion 96

The Pearly Gates 96

Side Saddle 96

The Y 97

Stairway to Heaven 97

Over the Edge 97

Best Kamasutra Positions for Anal Sex 97

The Pivot Position 97

Seesawing Position 97

The Buttering Position 98

The Hidden Door Position 98

The Caress of the Bud Position 98

The Seesaw Position 99

The Closed and Opened Ring Position 99

The Ripe Mango Plum Position 100

The Door Ajar Position 100

The Face to Face Position 100

The Top Position 100

Conclusion 101

DIRTY TALK 102

Introduction 102

What is Dirty Talk? 102

The Implications of Dirty Talking 104

The Effects of Dirty Talking 104

How to Talk Dirty 104

The Right Way 104

How To Turn Her On 105

(1) Make her feel good.. 106

(2) Seduce her with dirty talking........................... 106

(3) Tease her with aphrodisiacs 107

(4) Pamper her with a seductive massage 107

Five Tips to Start Dirty Talking 107

Be original 107

Be confident... 107

Keep it at bay 108

Have fun.. 108

Be yourself 108

Romance Tips For Your Girl................................ 108

1: Start slow 108

2: The perfect first kiss.................................... 109

3: Compliment her 109

4: Planning.. 109

5: Public Dirty Talking..................................... 109

6: Some 'her' time 109

7: Fireplaces 109

8: Cherish her completely 110

9: The necktie.. 110

10: Makeup sex 110

11: Gifts... 110

12: Take her shopping...................................... 110

13: Kiss her more often 110

15: Listen... 111

16: Make a fantasy box 111

17: Never buy carnations 111

18: Make her breakfast in bed 111

19: Never Hesitate 111

20: Be her friend 111

Bed Dirty Talking...112

Maximize Pleasure From Dirty Talking 113

Naughty Sex..114

Benefits of Dirty Talking 117

3 Golden "Rules" To Not Exaggerate 118

1. Always be in agreement 118

2. Set Your Stakes 119

3. No insults 119

Dirty Talk to Woman..119

Dirty Talk to Man 132

Dirty Talk Games...142

1st Tip. How To Prepare Her For Sex Games.......................................142

2nd Tip. How To Pick A Sex Game. 142

3rd Tip. How To Fully Enjoy It..143

4th Tip. Hot To Multiply Your Enjoyment Thereafter...........................143

Dirty Talk Examples 145

Conclusion 155

KAMASUTRA 156

What Is Kama Sutra 156

Meaning of Kama Sutra 156

The History Behind Kamasutra 157

The Social Ramifications Of The Kama Sutra.......................................157

From A Publishing Standpoint 157

The Kama Shastra Society 158

The Benefits of Kamasutra 158

The Kama Sutra Sex Positions 161

Standing Positions.. 161

The Fan.. 161

The Padlock 162

Luxurious Climb.. 163

The Royal Stairs 163

Standing on a wall 164

The visit 165

Let it Go.. 165

The butterfly 165

The Bracket 166

Special chair 166

The Mermaid.. 166

Scissors 168

The Climb 169

Sexy 5 169

The Hanging Woman.. 169

Right in target 169

The Apple 170

Standing up 171

Relaxing and Cuddling Positions 172

The French.. 172

The Vertical Hug 172

Simplicity.. 172

Front and back 174

The bell 175

Crisscross 176

Siesta in couple 177

The Laying Char 177

Orient secrets 177

Passionate Proposal.. 178

The pinwheel 179

The sandwich 180

The Lazy 2 181

Bonding.. 182

The Lazy Man... 182

The ascendant 183

The Joint 184

The Confession 184

Don't Go.. 184

Zen 185

Woman Dominates Positions 186

The Spanish... 186

Back View.. 186

Riding Backwards.. 187

Sitting face to tits... 188

The Amazon 188

The Sofa 190

The English Mount... 191

The tarantula 191

Bite her Hairs 191

Hot Rubbing.. 191

The Viking ride 191

The Steamer 192

Man Dominates Positions 194

Doggy Style.. 194

Legs on shoulder 195

Slipping... 196

The Candle 197

The Eight 199

Flexuosity 200

The Star 201

Bandoleer.. 202

Samba... 203

Look me in the eye 204

The Lateral Join 205

The Let's go home 205

Dirty Dance.. 205

The Sphinx... 205

Adoration 205

Nirvana.. 206

Lotus... 207

Indrani... 208

Utphallaka 209

The Magical Mountain 210

Odalisque 211

The Gold Triangle 211

Sitting positions... 212

Lotus... 212

The Magical Ride 213

Rocking horse 214

The Rocking Chair 215

The love chair 215

The Lazy Mermaid 215

The Limbo 215

The naughty 215

Acrobatic positions 217

The Y 217

The X 218

The Acrobats...219

Alternating legs 219

The boat..219

The Drawbridge 219

The Triumph Arc 221

Propeller 222

The Indian Headstand..223

Supernova..224

The monkey 225

Gravity 226

The Head Game 226

Pinball 226

The Clamp 226

The wheelbarrow..226

The wheelbarrow (alternative)..227

Conclusion 228

INTRODUCTION

Perhaps no other aspect of human life attracts as much attention and zeal as sex. And this curiosity is understandable and logical; most individuals want their romantic relationships to be as varied and harmonious as possible. Do you want your partner and you to have a flawless mutual understanding? Do you wish to be aware of your partner's as well as your own desires? Do you want to learn how to become an organic whole with your spouse and provide genuine pleasure to him or her? If you responded "yes" to at least one of these questions, then reading this book is the best decision you've ever made.

This book is recommended for both experienced couples and those who are just starting out in a relationship. It's for individuals who desire to use sexual union as a means of achieving spiritual love and freedom. And especially for those for whom love and trust are synonymous, who are willing to not only accept but also to give.

On the path to sexual peace and liberation, there are many complications, fallacies, and false moral prohibitions. This is unsurprising, given that we are all products of Western civilization. Meanwhile, the Eastern approach of sensuous love differs dramatically from Western sexual culture. The body and spiritual life, sexuality, and religiosity were once regarded to be one entity in Hinduism. The spiritual component of sex was addressed in all ancient oriental treatises on the art of love, and the Kama Sutra is possibly the most famous.

The Kama Sutra is an inspiring guide for millions of couples today, teaching them how to control their mind and body, emotions, and passion, allowing them to discover freedom and harmony in their intimate relationships.

We shall explain what the Kama Sutra is and where love and intimacy fit into it in this book. We'll also go over certain topics like foreplay and flirting, which will give you a lot of practical tips on how to keep your sensual attraction high. You will find a comprehensive arsenal of all sexual positions provided in the Kama Sutra by reading this book.

We'd like to introduce readers to mystical sexual rituals, orgasm-delaying techniques, oral sex, and other facets of sexuality. Our goal is to communicate the wisdom contained in the Kama Sutra in a simple and straightforward manner that is entirely adapted to the vision of the modern person.

From the first kisses and lovemaking to the secrets of a spectacular orgasm, this book takes you through all of the natural processes of sexual intercourse between a man and a woman. Your relationship will not become routine as a result of the variety of strategies and approaches featured in this book. On the other hand, you can continuously uncover new feelings that you have never felt before.

It will not be difficult to learn these techniques, and the end result will far exceed your expectations.

So, if you want to fully realize your sexual potential and become a relentless, incredibly innovative lover, this is the book for you!

HOW TO FLIRT AND SEDUCE

Flirting

In an almost forgotten past, probably the time of your grandparents or their parents and grandparents, courting was a serious affair. In fact, very serious. When a man saw a woman he liked, he didn't go straight to ask her out.

First, he would go to her parents or guardians and ask for permission to court her. When he would get permission, that's when the courtship officially began, in which the man calls the woman, comes to her home for a visit, and brings her flowers. This would go on and on as they would get to know each other - a process that could go on for months, even years.

In a nutshell, wooing is a period in a relationship that precedes engagement and marriage. It is a phase where people get to know each other better before deciding to take the relationship to the next level. Therefore, courtship is done when a boy is sure that the person, he wants to woo is someone to build a serious and lasting relationship with.

However, these days, this is difficult to do. Do you know for sure that the person they love is the one they really want to spend their life in any case? Therefore, courtship is actually not as simple as it seems, so that's probably why many don't care about it.

Flirting is a form of communication, of human interaction that takes place in the attraction phase, one of the initial moments of seduction in which you are evaluated as possible partners and in which you are judged at the same time. Immediately after approaching a girl, we move on to the attraction phase and through flirting we can continue or not our knowledge. During flirting you create a tantalizing game based on two fundamental aspects:

1) the unsaid: courtship occurs without openly revealing one's interest, everything must be understood and body language becomes essential to express our interest. Both of you are aware of what's going on, but it's not being said openly

2) the allusion continues to attraction and sex

Each of us has its own strategy, but there are some more effective behaviors than others. We will see some general tips to make flirting effective:

1) Look into each other's eyes. As we have seen, flirting is mainly based on non-verbal language, therefore eye contact is essential. Eye contact arouses strong emotions, so much so that if too much intensity is created, it is necessary to look away to avoid embarrassment and departure. This behavior must be maintained in the salient parts of the conversation, but if you want to snub the partner when he speaks, the gaze can be diverted

2) Joke. You can make funny jokes about episodes that you are aware of, make fun of yourself and use irony, without exaggerating. Communication must be light and playful. It is necessary to avoid too logical and personal topics (politics, religion, education) that could create a detachment in case of conflicting opinions, lighter subjects manage to convey more emotions because they are less demanding

3) Reduce interpersonal space. When two people are attracted, their distances are reduced. You have to approach it in a natural way in order to create more connection between you. The approach must be gradual, otherwise, it could have an opposite effect

4) Show security through body language, non-verbal language is characterized above all by how we distribute our body in space. You must show a safe attitude by avoiding crossing your arms and legs. We must keep the body positioned towards the other person. In case you want to remove attention, you can turn your head slightly in another direction

5) Seduce with physical contact, ideal contact during flirting should be neither too short nor too long to create awe. If you speak gesticulating, approaching, and creating a contact will seem a natural gesture.

In conclusion, it must be remembered that flirting starts one way and is transformed. The playful component is usually the initial one which is turning into a more sexual component. During the flirting phase, there must be an alternation between interest and disinterest in order to create a mechanism composed of mixed signals useful above all to confuse and create peaks of attraction. For example, you can go away with your body or look away and then fix yourself and get closer with your body. It is a "push and pull" in which attention is given and removed.

Basics of courtship and how to do it

Now, if you want to be all old-fashioned or the woman/man you like wants you to court her/him, then you should know the basics of courtship.

1 Be crystal. Unlike the ambiguity of dating, wooing means that you need to be clear about exactly what your intentions are. Tell that you like her/him and

want to woo her/him. Yes, you talk about "courtship" and she/he will surely pass out!

2 You know her/him. In essence, courting means knowing the deepest and best person. Aside from the traditional formality, the courtship is about two people who become good friends before deciding whether or not they are suitable.

If so, they take the relationship to the next level, which is a form of commitment. Today, this only happens when dating usually happens, and two people see each other exclusively.

3 The best foot forward. While being all good at this stage may be untrue, it helps not only be yourself but the better version of yourself.

This means making a little extra effort to not be easily pissed when the waiter messes up your orders at your date, or be more thoughtful about the things you don't like about the woman/man you're wooing.

4 Boundaries. What distinguishes courtship from dating are boundaries. With dating, people have a tendency to be more intimate with each other. Along with the tendency to go too fast in the relationship.

Flattery creates a boundary that must not be crossed. Anything close to kissing or taking out is not allowed, and two people are often limited to the company. At most holding hands and quick kisses on the cheek.

5 Longevity. It is common for someone who is in a relationship to not pursue the next level and fully engage with each other. Often, dating relationships don't really last.

However, with courtship, there is a fairly established period in which couples engage in the same activities similar to what dating does, such as going out, meeting friends, and many other things.

6 Friendship. Courtship often establishes the first friendship between two people before they take things to the next level. This is because courtship allows people to do things without the pressure of sleeping together. Give them enough chance to be together, be who they really are, and get to know each other.

Contrary to what you might think, courting is not that out of date. There are still men and women who love to woo and be wooed. If you are one of these, read these tips and have a better chance of making it yours

1 Make her/him feel attractive. While you have to respect the boundaries of courtship, this doesn't mean you can't express how attracted you are to her/him. Make her/him feel special with accurate and genuine compliments. You can also give her the usual flowers and chocolates, or make her/him pass out with love songs.

2 Write letters. What could be more romantic than bringing back the lost art of writing letters? Take imaginative stationery from a specialty card store and wipe the dust off your ballpoint pens.

Pen your thoughts, feelings, and aspirations about your budding relationship. You don't have to be Shakespeare, but eloquence and sincerity beat 140-character tweets at any time.

3 Revive cavalry. The women of these times are so tired of the idea that men are these knights in shining armor that they are fine without cavalry. In fact, there are within these neo-feminist women who believe they don't need a man to help them get through life.

Prove that she's wrong. Be chivalrous, you give her an unexpected and surprisingly pleasant surprise that makes you memorable and more tender than any other guy she may have met.

4 The date. Take her out for lunch, dinner, a walk in the park, a night at the museum, feed the pigeons and make it interesting every time you spend together. You are building memories with her/him and at the same time you invest time and effort to get to know yourself better.

5 Manage your expectations. Remember, don't expect a kiss, or even a few spasms, in exchange for everything you do. When you court, don't send her/him with checkers just to get in her pants, let's make it clear. You would sincerely want your intentions and sincerity to be known.

6 It's worth it. In a world where the instant is not even instantaneous enough for some, courting is like moving on the ladder of relationships. Add to that the many things you need to do for the woman/man you are trying to get to know, create trust, show commitment, and ultimately win her/his heart. This is called delayed gratification, which is not good for many these days.

Despite their denials, even the most exhausted woman or man would like to be treated like a queen or king. Do not hesitate to shower her with affection and gifts, as well as compliments, time, and commitment. Even your simplest efforts go far beyond your way of being faithful to your intentions.

INTIMACY: IMPORTANCE OF IT AND HOW TO PRACTICE

What is Intimacy

The word intimacy is frequently confused. Being intimate does not necessarily mean that you are having sex. There or a lot of sexual or physical acts that we participate in that actual house no intimacy at all. In this chapter, we are going to really get into the meat of what intimacy is. It affects us physically, mentally, and emotionally. When you have a good understanding of what intimacy is and what it means, your connection to your partner will be enhanced.

If you have a deep level of intimacy with another person, it also means that you know them on a different way than others. It is something that takes an extended period of time. You won't become truly intimate with another person through a simple conversation or in spending a single day together. Intimacy will grow over time, as both people work to nurture their relationship. When both parties understand that mistakes happen and they forgive each other so that they can continue on and learn, true intimacy starts to develop.

Intimacy can be unsettling for many individuals. This is because you have a deeper sense of closeness with someone when you are intimate with them than you do with others. Working over your fears will help you build a strong and healthy relationship.

Intimacy involves a variety of different key aspects. Each one will play a role in deepening the connection between you and your partner. This connection will allow you to be truly intimate with another person. Let's take a look at the different pieces that one put together equal true intimacy.

Tips

Some signs that the person you are interested in or starting a relationship with is not right for you are:

- They blame you with no accountability for their own actions
- They try and keep you from your other friends
- They are not supportive of your thoughts and ideas
- They get mad with no understanding when you try and discuss serious topics
- They try and control the way you think and feel
- They ignore your wants, needs, and desires
- They misinterpret what you say and twist it to use it against you
- It feels impossible to express yourself truthfully
- You feel as if you are not being heard when you talk
- There is little or no room for compromise

These are just a few of the signs that you should look for when entering into a new relationship to choose whether or not it is one that will be healthy for you.

Some things are more obvious to see than others. Taking the time to reflect on how your intended acts during serious situations can help you gain insight as to what a future with them may look like. Remember that while people change slightly throughout their lives, for the most part, they are who they are, and if they are right for you, you won't be thinking about their potential.

When we start a new relationship, we start to learn about the good and bad sides of a person. Showing yourself and exposing what you truly believe is a step in the right direction when trying to attain a truly intimate relationship. Know that when you express yourself in a raw way, the reaction may not be what you expect. Obviously, you want your partner to be understanding and supportive, but remember that it goes both ways. So, when they are expressing themselves, think about your reactions and how it is affecting the person you are developing feelings for.

Taking the time to look at your differences is very important. It can help you understand if the relationship is worth moving forward with. Some differences can help us grow and evolve while others can be complete deal-breakers. Finding these things out, in the beginning, can help you avoid heartache and wasting your time.

Being emotionally mindful is another component in building intimacy with your partner. How we express, ourselves plays a role in helping or hurting the level of intimacy we experience. At one time or another, will happen that it is likely that you are going to have negative feelings toward your partner, this is normal, taking the time to consider how you should express them is really the important part.

You should trust your partner so that you can be honest with them, but you also need to be mindful of what you are saying. The words we use can cut deeply and cause the connection between the two of you to suffer. If you explode or become nasty because of heightened emotions, it could push your partner away and also lead to the demise of the relationship. So, be understanding and think before you speak to ensure that you and your lover stay closely connected and will be able to work through issues together.

Last, but not least, when working on nurturing your level of intimacy, work on being the best version of yourself. If you think that qualities like compassion, faithfulness, generosity, and understanding are important in a relationship, then work on being all of those things. No one is perfect, and we all have things to work on, but doing our best by someone else helps to make us worthy of intimacy. Also, be willing to listen to their opinion and the feedback they give you on your thoughts.

Physical and Sexual Intimacy

Physical intimacy is not necessarily just sex; it is when we are affectionate with our partner. It includes things like holding hands, kissing, hugging, and cuddling. There should be a great physical connection when you are trying to achieve great levels of intimacy. When you are physical, in any way, with your partner, think about how it makes you feel. Are they good reactions or bad ones? By answering this simple question, it can become quite easy to see if this is the person you should be connecting with or not.

When we are intimate on a mental level, it means that we can easily express our thoughts and ideas about everything with another person. When we have the ability to truly share what is on our mind, it is going to enable us to become vulnerable with our partner. We trust them and, in turn, share all things with them. Their reactions are considerate, and we feel as if we have been heard. Connection on this mental level is a key element in true intimacy and a healthy relationship.

Emotional intimacy is probably one of the scariest forms for a lot of people. When you choose to be emotionally open, allowing your partner to see the lightest and darkest sides of you, it can be intimidating. However, when trust has been built, and lines of communication are open and honest, it really isn't as scary as many people think. True emotional intimacy will allow you to share your joy as well as your sorrow with another person. They will be there to support you whether you are feeling high on life or exceptionally low.

When you combine all three types of intimacy, you are looking at it in its most pure form. Reaching these levels of intimacy does not happen with every relationship, and it certainly does not happen overnight. In fact, it can only be accomplished in those relationships that are consistently worked on. When you find the person who you can open up to on every level, and that is willing to do the same with you, it is worth the effort. With continued effort, respect, openness, and caring, intimacy can truly solidify you as a couple and ensure your relationship is one that is healthy and happy in every area.

Humans are the species where sexuality is the most influenced by the quality of the relationship. In human beings, sexual stimulation is made up of several factors and not simply the excitement of the senses. Sensory touch and then sight, taste, smell, and hearing are the elements that contribute to sexual arousal. But how everyone feels about their feelings and how they get them has a more significant impact on excitement than sensory stimulation.

Your feelings may have a more significant influence on genital function and orgasm than physical sensations. So the overall sexual stimulation needed to reach the stimulation threshold of excitement and then orgasm is given by the sensory stimulation that you receive from your partner plus your sensations and thoughts (on what you are doing, with who is doing it, and what it implies for itself).

Sex thus becomes a thermometer of the relationship one has with oneself and with the other, the mood with which a connection is faced, the evaluation of the sexual encounter (the meaning of the sexual experience may or may not be in agreement with who you are), unresolved emotional problems, being able to maintain the right atmosphere in the room where you are but also in your head and anxiety, all influence in determining the pleasantness or otherwise of the relationship.

THE BASIS OF FOREPLAY

The foreplay is a set of emotionally and physically intimate acts between two or more people meant to create sexual arousal and desire for sexual activity. The foreplay is what warms the environment and leads to sex. Its primary purpose is to generate excitement and prepare the two partners to make love.

We are all captivated by the sex scenes of the films, by the garments that fly conspicuously all around, and by the bodies that rapidly end up between the sheets. In the collective imagination, this is cool and sometimes might happen, but in most cases, everything starts before, in a moderate and fragile way, without all the display. When foreplay was worked out in the original Kama Sutra, there was a reference to the servants who might help the man arrange the room before meeting with his lady. Many of us do not have workers that we can depend on to do these things for us in the present society. It is now more connected with modern society than to the Indian culture of a few centuries ago. Hopefully, you will find here some interesting ideas for your foreplay.

Erogenous Zones

Tease your partner with light hands, from feet to head, listening to his reactions. Do not forget the erogenous zones: the breasts or nipples (even those of him are sensitive), the inside of the thighs, the buttocks, the back of the knees, the ears. Do not be fierce or get offended if the partner shows impatience or remains insensitive to certain touches. Just try it another way.

The human being needs to kiss and be kissed, especially before and during sex. Why? The frequency and intensity of contact between lovers' mouths is a thermometer to measure the degree of intimacy and health of the couple. With a French kiss, messages of sexual pleasure are sent to the brain through the nerve endings on the surface of the tongues. For this reason, psychologists consider language to be a psychological sexual organ, that is, a part of the body that plays a fundamental role in love affairs, even though it is not involved in reproduction.

The sexual organs can be stimulated with the hands, the mouth, or by rubbing (masturbation). The most sensitive female point is the clitoris, an erectile body that has many nerve endings, between the folds of the labia minora, and which for a significant percentage of women represents the only viaticum for pleasure (clitoral orgasm). Many women, however, experience pain if at the beginning the stimulation is direct: therefore it is advisable to start from the surrounding area, slowly, and always in a gentle way. Thousands of pleasure receptors are concentrated in the penis, the male genital organ: for example the crown, the skin circumference that separates the rod from the glans penis (the top of the penis), which is a very sensitive area, or the glans itself. The testicles are also an erogenous zone. During foreplay some people prefer silence, others love to pronounce or hear words of love, and still, others get excited with hard sentences.

Bottoms of feet
Feet have been the object of desire for a century. Some people love them, and some people hate them. Regardless of whether you are a foot lover or not, it is essential to know that feet have multiple nerve ends and pressure points; stimulating this often-neglected area with a massage or a soft touch can lead to pleasurable sensations.

Armpits
Inner arms and armpits are susceptible areas where many people are touchy. You can use a soft touch along this area to stimulate the nerves and ignite the flame. Why not play with a feather and torment your partner? Based on their body's response, you can mix tickling and sexual arousal.

Neck
The neck is one of the most famous and sensitive erogenous zones, from the nape at the back to the sides below the jawline. Many people enjoy stimulation along the neck with a light touch or kissing.
Lower stomach and belly button
The lower abdomen and belly button are susceptible areas, and they have the advantage of being near the genital region. A light touch near these areas can easily lead to sexual arousal.

Behind the knee
This area might come as a surprise, but there is another sensitive, nerve-rich body area behind the knee. In most cases, these areas are overlooked, but trust me; paying particular attention to it during a full-body massage can elicit arousal.

Ears

The ears are full of nerves and sensory receptors, and they are one of the most sensitive erogenous zones in the human body. No single spot from the tip to the lob will not elicit arousal.

You can play with them in various ways; light nibbles or kisses are a good ice breaker, and, depending on what your partner likes, you could bite even a bit harder or suck them.

Hands

Hands, like feet, have many nerve endings that can be stimulated during foreplay. Fingertips and palms are particularly sensitive to licking and kissing. Slowly sucking a finger or kissing it can be incredibly sexy; also, as a bonus, the man's mind tends to associate sucking a finger with fellatio.

Inner thighs

The inner thighs are incredibly close to genital areas and particularly sensitive. You can try a light touch while moving towards the genitals; your partner will love it!

Genital region

Genitals are the most known erogenous zones and the ultimate source of sexual arousal.

For men, you can focus on the head (or glans) of the penis, the frenulum (the underneath skin where the shaft plus the head meet), the foreskin (for uncircumcised men), the scrotum, the perineum (the skin separating the penis and anus), and the prostate (stretched inside the rectum).

For women, you can focus on the pubic mound, the clitoris, the G-spot (two to three inches internal, on the front vaginal wall), the A-spot (four to five inches inside, on the frontal vagina wall), and the cervix.

Let's see in more detail the woman's genital region.

The labia are now and again alluded to as the "lips" of a lady's private parts.

We can split a lady's private parts into external labia, covering the internal labia, the clitoris, and the vagina. These areas contain many sensitive spots, which make them exceptionally touchy to contact and can, in this manner, give the lady colossal pleasure when stimulated correctly. The labia can be animated by a man's pelvic district or the base of his penis when he is penetrating her or giving her oral sex by utilizing his mouth and tongue. Fingers or hands can also stimulate them during foreplay or when the man uses his hands to invigorate the lady's privates.

The clitoris is the way to pleasure a lady. The clitoris is now and again alluded to as the female penis since, when a lady turns out to be sexually stirred, her clitoris will load up with blood and swell, making it increment in size like the penis of a male. When this occurs, you can consider it a female erection. That means the extending or erection of the clitoris makes it considerably more delicate than it ordinarily would be, which prompts sensations of sexual excitement and pleasure when it is correctly stimulated. Doing this for quite a while in the correct manner can lead to orgasm.

The vagina is another touchy spot on a lady that can give her incredible sensations of pleasure when genuinely stimulated. The vagina is a trench situated between a lady's legs, prompting her uterus inside her body. The dividers of the vagina contain a few places that, when stimulated, will initiate profound orgasms for the lady.

The G-Spot is one of the spots inside the vagina that can give a lady orgasm. That spot can be stimulated with the man's penis during penetration or with fingers.

There are certain situations for the ideal points of penis-to-vagina that produce the G-Spot incitement, and we will take a gander at these later in this book. For the time being, note that the G-Spot will prompt an exceptionally incredible and amazingly pleasurable orgasm for the lady when stimulated. The specific spot should be produced repeatedly as her pleasure builds right until it reaches a peak, and she orgasms.

Nipples

The nipples and the areolas (or the skin around the nipples) are incredibly sensitive hotspots on the body and are closely tied to the sensations in the genitals. Many people vary widely in the sensitivity of their nipples—some are too sensitive to enjoy marvels, while others want rougher play, such as biting or nipple clamps. Each lady is diverse in how delicate her areolas are, yet numerous ladies can turn out to be sexually stirred by having their areolas stimulated. Nipples are an excellent spot to begin the foreplay; these parts are sensible and, with the proper stimulation, can turn on a woman in a few minutes. It has been estimated that a few ladies are even ready to arrive at orgasm through areola incitement. Remember that she might be one of those!

Scalp

The scalp has many delicate nerve endings, which is why scalp massages can be delightful. Gentle massaging or hair pulling can activate these nerves and send pleasurable sensations throughout the body.

BEST WAYS FOR FOREPLAY

Different Types of Kisses

In the original version of the Kama Sutra, there are described a series of kisses that can be used in various situations. Nowadays, some of them might seem obvious, but we must consider that centuries ago, there was no sex education or media to obtain this information.

Measured kiss
When one person offers their lips but does not move them, it is called a measured kiss. While the other person remained passive, the other presses their lips against theirs, kissing the mouth. This kiss can still be passionate, especially if you're experimenting with who's the boss.

Throbbing kiss
According to the Kama Sutra, the throbbing kiss is generally initiated by the ladies, and males are the receivers. This kiss starts with bringing the lips close to your partner's mouth and gently press the lips against her lips. While the lady can touch her partner's lips with her hands or slowly with her tongue, her lower lip slowly moves to suck on his lips. At this point, the lower lip does the real action. This is a very passionate kiss, perfect for foreplay and sexual act.

Askew kiss
Askew kiss is perhaps the most widely recognized kiss for lovers to attempt. It happens when the two accomplices tilt their heads into one another as they press their mouths together. This position ensures that the noses do not disrupt the general flows while the tongues have the freedom to move inside the partner's mouth. This type of kiss is also called 'the crosswise,' and it is perfect for enthusiastic kisses.

Bent kiss
This kiss is also known as the 'turned kiss' and is probably one of the most romantic kisses in the Kama Sutra. The bent kiss is when one partner takes the chin of their lover and tilts it up towards them to kiss the lips. You can intensify this kiss by holding your partner's face. The Bent Kiss is ideal for foreplay as you are driving your accomplice towards more prominent sexual release.

Direct kiss
This kiss is also known as the 'equal kiss' as the two partners are on an equal playing field. You are face to face to your partner and kisses, licks, and sucks each other's lips. The tongue can be included in these kissing games. You can also compete with your partner assigning the victory to "the person who first gets the lower lip of the other."

33

Pressure kiss

The pressure kiss may appear aggressive, but quite a lot of people enjoy it. This kiss incorporates biting and keeping the mouth and the lips of your accomplice closed. Therefore, it is imperative to do it only briefly to don't hurt them. To keep the passion flowing, you can also make a circle with your fingers and kiss them against your partner's lips; this will also help reduce the pressure if needed.

Top kiss

This kiss produces delicious sensations, as the top kiss includes one lover kissing the upper lip of the other. While this occurs, the other accomplice can kiss the lower lip, making them tingle all over.

Distraction kiss

This kiss is mentioned in the original Kama Sutra and makes its purpose clear with only its name. It is used to draw your partner's attention. This kiss, however, should not be limited to the mouth. It can affect also other parts, such as the face, ear, neck, chest, and any of a man's or woman's erogenous zones.

Clip kiss

The clip kiss is where one partner touches the other's tongue or lips with their tongue, causing a "battle of tongues," which can be very pleasurable for both. This is a profoundly passionate type of kiss but, according to the original book, this kiss can also show immaturity.

Stirring kiss

Stirring kiss is the most tender and sweet kiss. One accomplice kisses the other sweetly but firmly to kindle their passion. The original Kama Sutra doesn't contain a lot of details regarding this type of kiss. It suggests a woman doing this to her lover while they are sleeping. It is a demonstration of love and romance.

Contact kiss

The contact kiss is perfect for a steamy sex prelude. During this kiss, one accomplice provocatively and gently touches the other's mouth with their lips, and there's light yet extraordinary contact; it is brief but exciting.

Kiss to ignite the flame

The kiss ignites the flame when one lover returns to awake the other with a kiss at night. Here is when you perceive how sexual politics have changed throughout the centuries. The original text is vague but makes us consider the importance of consent. It says the lady might want to pretend still to be asleep to "find her lover's mood."

Eyelash kiss
Those with long eyelashes love this sort of kiss from the Kamasutra; the eyelash kiss is when you caress and touch your accomplice's lips with your eyelashes.

Finger kiss
The kiss with a finger is energizing from start to finish, as one accomplice places your finger in the other's mouth, takes it out, and brushes it across other lips. This kiss makes it an ideal introduction to oral sex.

Reflecting kiss
There are kisses that can show desire and love without kissing your partner. That type of kiss is when you see the reflection of your partner in a mirror or in water to show how seriously you want them. This kiss is like a transferred kiss that might involve kissing a picture or a statue and transferring the love to an inanimate object. It's very similar to when teenagers kiss the posters of their idols hanging in their bedrooms.

Scratching
The art of scratching has its own section in the original Kama Sutra. There are tons of different ways to scratch your lover and spice up your relationship. Here I am listing my interpretation of the most common scratching techniques reported in the original text.

Sounding
Sounding is a soft scratching that does not leave any marks. When a person scratches the chin, the breasts, the lower lip, or the Jaghana (the loin; the buttocks) of another so softly, it makes the partner's hair stand up. The nails themselves make a sound, called a 'sounding or pressing with the nails.'

Half Moon
This scratch leaves a curved mark with the nails that resembles a 'half-moon.' It is usually impressed on the neck and the breasts or other sensitive body parts of your partner.

Circle
A circle is made by two half-moons created beside each other. This mark with the nails is generally made on the navel, the small cavities about the buttocks, and the thigh joints.

Line
This is probably the simplest type of scratch. It is made in the shape of a small line and can be applied to any part of the body.

Tiger's Nail
A curved scratch, usually made on the breast, is called a 'tiger's nail.'

Peacock's Foot
This type of scratch requires a great deal of skill to make it properly. The 'Peacock's Foot' is a curved mark made by pressing all five nails into the breast. It requires a lot of practice to apply the same pressure with all five fingers and leave five perfect curved marks.

The Jump of a Hare
The 'Jump of a Hare' is realized when five marks with the nails are made close to one another near the nipple of the breast.

Leaf of a Blue Lotus
This mark is made in the shape of a lotus near the breast. It is designed to be placed in hidden locations across the body, particularly on the breast, so they are only seen by the two lovers and by no one else. They are there to remind their lover and excite them whenever they gaze upon each mark.

Eight bites of love
We discussed embraces, scratches, kisses, but what about biting? Biting is probably one of the most exciting art explained in the Kama Sutra; if done correctly can lead your partner to immeasurable pleasure. There is a bite suitable for every situation; the important thing is to know which one.

Gudhaka
Gudhka is the lightest of bites, and it is typically applied only to the lower lip and does not leave any imprint. It is intended to be a careful bite to be used during the foreplay.

Uchhunaka
A Uchhunaka, or dazzled bite, usually leaves a weak imprint. This bite focuses on a famous erogenous zone, the ears. It can also be executed on the left cheek. It is not intended as a single bite; when performing the Uchhunaka, you want to slowly and repeatedly bite the ears of your partner while reaching with your hands the sensible areas of their body. This bite shows control, and it is typically used during the foreplay when it is almost time to move to the sexual act.

Bindu
The Bindu (a small speck), like the Uchhunanka, is an elaborate bite. Other than the ears and cheeks, the "solitary bite" could also be made on the brow.

But, again, the lover needs to nip the skin so shrewdly that the imprint is only the size of a sesame seed.

Bindu Mala
The Bindu Mala are multiple bites usually made in circles on various parts of the body. Areas, where Bindu Mala can be applied, are neck, bosoms, empty of the tights. Using a Bindu Mala requires a lot of experience; the final goal is to create patterns resembling necklaces, bracelets, or jewelry with these marks.

Pravalamani
Pravalamani is a type of bite applied using the upper teeth or the upper incisors. The objective is to leave a little, decorative curved imprint on your partner. A Pravalamani mark resembles a half-moon due to the precision required to execute this type of mark. Due to the precision required, it is suggested not to perform this bite during sexual acts. Instead, use Pravalamani during the foreplay or in a moment of relaxation when you are still in complete control of your body.

Mani Mala
Mani Mala is very similar to the Bindu Mala, but in this case, the "necklaces" created have more extensive "corals" -the bite-size is slightly bigger-. Usually you can do that to breasts and tights.

Khandabhraka
Khandabhrakas are "clouds" of small bites scattered across the body without a particular arrangement. It is pretty common to apply these marks under the breasts, and due to the spontaneity of these patterns, this type of bite can be easily used during sexual acts.

Varaha Charvita
Varaha Charvita, also called chewing of the wild boar, is a variation of Khandabhrakas where the marks are closer and redder in the center. These bites are placed randomly and made in a state of great excitement during the sexual act. Compared to the other types of bites, Varaha Charvita and Khandabhrakas require less control and precision and, for this reason, are perfect to be executed during the sexual act.

Sucking the mango fruit: fellatio techniques
The Kama Sutra presents different fellatio techniques; in this chapter, I will summarize the most interesting. These can be used both during the foreplay but also are perfect for the sexual congress or the grand finale!

Touching
According to the original Kama Sutra text, touching, or Nimitta, is: "When your lover catches your penis in her hand and, shaping her lips to an 'O', lays them lightly to its tip, moving her head in tiny circles."

Nominal Congress
This technique is based on holding the penis in a single hand while placing your lips on it. The only -slow- movement is done with your mouth and tongue, and the focus is mainly on the gland.

Biting the Sides
With this technique, your fingers are used to cover the gland and slowly massage it while you then kiss and bite along the shaft.

Kissing
This is just a warmup technique where you hold the penis in the hand while covering it in kisses.

Rubbing
Remarkably like kissing, this occurs when you use your tongue and lick all over the penis until it is fully erected.

Sucking a Mango Fruit
Putting only half of the penis in the mouth and sucking on it

Swallowing Up
This is when the entire penis is placed in the mouth and down towards the back of the throat.

Outer Pincers
With this technique, you take the head of the penis gently between your lips, by turns pressing, kissing it tenderly, and pulling at its soft skin: this is "Bahiha-Samdansha" (the Outer Pincers).

Inner Pincers
This is the follow-up of the Outer Pincers technique. You allow the head to slide entirely into your mouth and press the shaft firmly between your lips, holding a moment before pulling away; it is called "Antaha-Samdansha" (the Inner Pincers).

Let your senses evolve
During the demonstration of lovemaking, a considerable lot of us will zero in on just the feeling of touch. We are distracted, essentially, by what adoring our accomplices feels like.

Yet shouldn't something be said about the other senses. What are you seeing? While the feeling of touch is so alive during our sexual experiences, what we see is likewise loaded with enchantment. Our accomplices are wonderlands of creaturely magnificence. We need to recognize the truth about that and add it to our sensual collection. As they burn through our accomplices with appreciation, our eyes are an under-used sense in the actual domain of the faculties – sexuality. You might think that men are more visual than ladies; experience has instructed me that this is not the case. Ladies have similarly a strong enthusiasm for what they see as men do. Men may locate this hard to accept, yet ladies' eyes see you for the sexy animals you are!

Our feeling of smell is overwhelmingly significant because it plays in causing us to select our partners. Even if we are not even aware of it, pheromones influence what attracts us to each other. The pheromonal aroma does not enroll with us, however, in a conscious way. What does, is the exceptional aroma of our accomplices the fragrance their skin conveys, and, in any event, when vigorously perfumed, this aroma can be distinguished. This is the reason we sniff their pillows when they are away from us. This peculiar fragrance is such a lot of a piece of those we share our love with that reminds us of them and the love we share with them. In sex, this scent can have a significant impact on desire and passion, as the action of our chemicals is increased and drive passion.

Suppose you are interested in exploring your senses further. In that case, the chapter "Sensory deprivation" of this book will contain more details and ideas on how you can enhance your senses during sex.

HOW TO MAKE FOREPLAY LAST LONG

Very often the foreplay is underestimated, it does not last long and the aim is to get straight to the point of penetration. Yet, whatever your partner may say, petting should last much longer. But how do you extend the foreplay? There are several tricks: firstly carry on the foreplay throughout the day, this does not mean that you will have to spend the whole day in underwear, but that you can stimulate your partner with a message, with a whispered phrase in the ear, with a provocative dress, with a mischievous joke. To extend the foreplay, also start by giving your partner or having him do a relaxing massage, which will make the atmosphere warm. If he tends to get to the point, take control of the situation, dictate the pace, guide the relationship: you will see that your partner will not mind your initiative. And then talk, do not keep inside what goes on in your head, in sex you must not have modesty, the more you will give space to your fantasies and the more the petting and the whole sexual relationship will be satisfying for both.

For those who desire to continue longer in bed and deliver more pleasure to their partner during your sexual experience, it should come as no surprise that slowing things way down is one of the most effortless ways to accomplish this end. Very often, we treat sex as an afterthought. If we have time, we might squeeze it into our days somewhere or perhaps before bed if we're not too tired. With this mentality, sex is only a rare treat, or maybe a chore to be endured, rather than a significant avenue of bonding and experiencing transcendental pleasure with your partner.

The health of one's relationship is every bit as important in one's life as one's physical, mental, and emotional health. When our love lives are not in harmony, it throws everything else out of whack, too. A peaceful and loving relationship, on the other hand, can bring peace and healing when all else has gone awry.

Because our relationships are such a central part of our lives, we owe our partners to handle them as a priority rather than an afterthought. One of the great insights about life is knowing that we have time for what we make time for. Permit yourself to slow down, knowing that you and your partner deserve the most entire and most pleasure-packed experience that is possible for you.

Extending Foreplay and Slowing Sex
Our culture has groomed us to be highly goal-oriented in our sex. The quest for the big "O" has captured our imaginations and provided content for dozens of self-help books, blogs, and advice magazines. But what if the constant striving for orgasm is all wrong?

Have you ever spent days searching for something that you lost? You scoured all the rooms in your house, picked over every inch of your car, retraced all your steps, and asked everyone you knew who may have seen the lost item. But all this was to no avail. No matter how much time you consumed searching and how close to the madness you drove yourself looking for this thing, it stayed lost. Finally, you accepted defeat and moved on, almost forgetting about the item entirely until one day when, as you were looking for something else, or perhaps not even looking at all, the long-lost item finally reappears.

Transcendental orgasms can be as elusive as the things we lose. The harder we strive for them, the less luck we will have in reaching them. When we let ourselves slow down and stop looking, however, this is precisely when we find exactly what we've been wanting.

40

Extending foreplay is very easy to do. The only limitation is your imagination. Your foreplay can be as sensual, as erotic, or as playful as you wish (though the best foreplay often embodies all of these elements).

Slowing down sex means literally that—slow down your movements. Fast and rough sex can feel amazing, but it is precisely the fastness of sexual activities that leads to quick orgasms. Our bodies can only handle so much stimulation before they need to give in. That doesn't mean that you need to do away with fast and rough sexual movements entirely; it simply means introducing more slow and deliberate movements into the mix.

Slow down the moment of initial penetration entirely, taking the time to look deeply into your partner's eyes and savor every ounce of sensation that comes from your first pairing. You will find that the emotional feelings that wash over you with this change are every bit as intense as the physical sensations.

Once you are connected, use slow and sensual movements throughout your lovemaking. Embrace your partner, caress their face and body, run your fingers up and down their back, kiss their neck and shoulders. Engage the whole body in the lovemaking process. If you feel the urge to climax before you are both ready, stop and take a few deep breaths until the urge subsides somewhat. You build a reserve of energy that will erupt and shake through your body when you decide to release it by delaying the moment of gratification.

Slowing down sex and touching your partner throughout the process will engage your whole body in the sexual experience. Most of us are used to concentrating on our genitals during sex because, of course, that is where the most sensation is happening. However, our skin is a susceptible organ covering our whole body, providing more potential for intense pleasure. Why limit your focus to only a tiny fraction of your body when you can feel joy throughout all of it?

Slow down your movements, engage your entire body, and connect with your partner deeply throughout your sexual experience. You will be astounded by the new levels of pleasure that you unleash.

Exploring Your Partner
How well do you and your partner know one another's bodies? Do you do everything that they like and don't like? Do they? How much do you know about what you genuinely like and don't like? If no one has ever caught the time to touch every part of your body and try every kind of touch, how will you ever have the opportunity to know everything that turns you off or on?

41

Foreplay is not only for pleasure, but it is also a form of communication. Engaging in extended foreplay is a conversation between you and your partner, a beautiful dance of giving and receiving that we can experience no other way. Sex and foreplay provide us with an unprecedented opportunity to get to know ourselves and our companions in a means that no one else does, deepening our bond in the relationship and elevating that bond to the level of sacred.

Take the time to explore your partner slowly and allow your partner to examine you. Just as they say, "life is about the journey, rather than the destination," so is sex, a beautiful journey of intimacy and sensual pleasure for you and you're beloved. Be very mindful about the sensations taking place in your own body as your lover touches, teases, kisses, and caresses you. Soak in every moment of pleasure, every tackle, and every chill that shakes your body. Practicing this level of mindfulness can be a deeply meditative process that improves your connection with your body, lowers your stress, and helps to clear your mind of worry and anxiety.

Practice a similar level of mindfulness as you explore your partner's body. Pay attention to every sigh, every moan, every giggle, and shiver. You will learn your partner's most sensitive areas, which make them squirm with desire and pleasure, and which they would prefer you stay away from. Gaze deeply into their eyes to connect your souls. Taste their skin beneath your lips. Feel the different textures of their skin. Absorb every beautiful and fleeting detail of these precious moments with your beloved and hold them within your heart and mind. They will be with you always.

Engage in All-Over Foreplay for an Enhanced Sexual Experience

Just as with sex, we often spend foreplay focusing on our genitals, nipples, and other hot spots. As we saw earlier, however, the whole surface of the body holds the potential to experience an incredible amount of pleasure. The rushed and goal-oriented approach to sex that so many of us take compels us to take this narrow focus and neglect the rest of our bodies. Our drive for instant gratification robs us of our chance to surprise and delight ourselves on increasingly more profound and more exotic levels.

The difference between typical sex and Tantric sex is often compared to fast food and a gourmet, multiple-course meal. The gourmet meal takes longer to prepare, but it is much healthier and ultimately more satisfying and delicious for those who take the time to prepare it. Similarly, slow and sensual sex preceded by long, steamy foreplay is a thousand times more satisfying than rushed sex.

As you and your partner explore one another's bodies, you will naturally find more pleasurable areas when stimulated than others. However, it is essential to avoid the lure to focus exclusively on these areas while ignoring the rest of the body.

Kissing your partner's whole body is a beautiful and sensual way to bring pleasure to you both. When you do this, take the time to lick and even gently nibble on different parts of their skin.

You can also tease them with a feather or other object. The light tickle will arouse and delight them as you run it over the different parts of their body, awakening their skin and sending shivers through their body.

A full-body massage is a beautiful way to nurture your partner and help them relax. We hold stress in places we never even realize until they are touched and massaged. Massaging your partner can help them to find these stress points and begin to release their tension, bringing them both sensual delight as well as gentle healing.

Slowing down with sex and foreplay is not only a powerful way to enhance and prolong the sensual experience, but it is also a way to communicate your deep love and care for your partner. When you take things slow, explore one another, and give all-over pleasure, you transform your lovemaking into a profoundly intimate and nurturing experience that can bring enormous healing to you as individuals and to the relationship as a whole.

WHAT IS TANTRIC SEX

It is a practice born in India around 400 B.C. and its aim has always been the knowledge and maturation of oneself. At that time, sexuality was in fact used to unite with the other and to ignite the spark of a person's nature. The word "tantra" is of Sanskrit origin, meaning principle, essence, technique and was used to indicate a series of spiritual teachings and esoteric traditions born in Indian religious cultures. As time went by, the term began to indicate that set of "sacred" sexual practices and rituals listed in Tantric literature that allow the body and mind to free themselves and experience almost supernatural sensations. In today's society, where sexuality is experienced more with the head than with the body, Tantric sex teaches the importance of slowness, attention, naturalness and complicity, all characteristics that deepen intimacy and increase passion, allowing you to communicate openly and authentically with your partner. Unlike traditional sex, in tantric sex it is essential to leave out the anxiety of orgasm, performance, result and you have to learn to enjoy eroticism in its totality, from sounds to breaths, up to movements.

Try to think about the typical sex, without romance: that's what you do quickly, with him often coming before her, few glances and many fixed thoughts. Will he see that I have cellulitis? Do I have it long enough for her? We are light years away from the concept of tantric sex, of slow and overwhelming spiritual and physical union that we all dream of as teenagers. You have surely heard of tantric sex thanks to some stars (Sting, anyone?), but few really know what they are talking about.

It's a real philosophy that tells us how to learn how to have sex for hours, how to prolong the pleasure to infinity and how to experience an extreme orgasm. Or not to feel it at all, discovering another level of pleasure where you don't need a sudden peak of sensations (incredible, but true!). If you are looking for a way to turn your sexual experiences as a couple into something supernatural, then we explain everything there is to know about tantra for two. And goodbye #frever to bad sex.

Tantric sex is recommended only for people who are particularly close because it is a more mental than physical practice that brings out all the problems and psychological motivations that are the basis of a relationship. At the same time, it is a practice that fights routine and allows you to create a deep, passionate connection, a real spiritual enlightenment. To deal with it in the best way, first of all, one should not be afraid to try something new. Only with an open mind and an open heart can you achieve total enjoyment. Then, you must decide to devote at least one hour a week to your sexuality, even when you are tired or stressed.

Tantric sex is in fact able to invigorate the body and make it stronger and more energetic. In addition, the atmosphere is very important to reach the peak of pleasure: the bedroom must be a magical space, a temple of love, a real feast of the senses. So it is good to decorate the bed with pillows, blankets, flowers, incense and even some fruit and some drinks. At this point, you will be able to relax, removing any blockages or tension that prevents the body to feel a deep and intense pleasure.

In tantric sex it is important to sit in front of your partner and meditate together with him, connecting your breath and your heart with that of the other. Although it may seem like a weird practice, once you try the positions of tantra the pleasure will turn into a real bliss. Tantric sex is a discipline open also to homosexuals, who can practice a sensual erotic massage to their partner. Such an intimate moment can make you rediscover your body and reach an extreme pleasure. Homosexuality in the East has never been considered a taboo and that's why such a passionate and intense sexual practice is open to any kind of gender.

The True Story Of Tantra - What Is And What Is Not

The original Tantra, also known as "Red" or "left hand" is linked to ancient matriarchal societies and has as its center the feminine energy. While the Tantra called "White" or "Right Hand", created later due to Muslim infiltration, derives from Indian patriarchal societies, as is the current Western one.

The difference between Red Tantra and White Tantra is radical. The second, White Tantra, is based on static and solitary meditations, while Red Tantra is a practice in which meditation is not only immobility and seriousness. In Red Tantra, meditation and sacredness are lived in every moment of existence, through deep listening and attention to what happens inside and outside of us. Meditation happens while dancing, working, hugging, eating, drinking, playing and talking.

There is a lot of confusion about what Tantra really is and especially a lot of targeted misinformation because of the persecution to which Original Tantra was subject. Tantra carries with it the burden of false clichés, such as free sex.

Unlike other disciplines that have been less polluted, Tantra is for many a kind of Yoga practice; for others an orgiastic practice and for others a religion.

Summing up the only true Tantra is the one called Red. This does not mean that Tantra yoga, the white one and the one of the right hand, cannot be useful tools; but if you practice them you should at least know that you are not doing Tantra.

The Origins

According to the almost unanimous opinion of scholars, the archaic nature of the Red Tantra dates back to pre-Vedic cultures, to the very beginnings of Indian history, identifiable with the Harappei, Sindhu and other Dravidian populations who developed their Indus Valley civilization. According to some in the third millennium B.C. these populations were spread in a huge territory that went from Spain to the valley of the Ganges. Their precursors had settled in the Indus valley in Mehrgar starting from 7000 BC and their traces can be found until 5500 BC.

The Dravidian populations, therefore, appeared there around 6000-5000 B.C., had their apogee between 2300 and 1300 B.C. and disappeared, rather quickly, in a period of 100 years between 1900 and 1800 B.C. The reasons for their disappearance were attributed in the past to invasions of the Aryan population from the north. Today it tends to be attributed rather to a tectonic movement that raised the Aravali hills in the north of Rajastan, depriving the river that supported the Dravida civilization (the Ghaggar-Hakra) of most of its tributaries.

The Harappei population showed a strong interest in the arts and welfare. Theirs was a matriarchal society, the most important central monument of their city, was a large swimming pool; the element water was fundamental in their society and since then there was already a bath in every house. The woman was at the center of culture, centered on the mother goddess. The female figure dominated the sanctuaries and with open arms and legs, she offered herself for adoration. The Harappei used to keep a large bed in the center of the most important room of the house and they practiced Tantra. Their religion was closely related to the body, well-being and sexuality.

It can be said that Red Tantra is the expression of all those practices that include sexuality. Red Tantra includes practices that also occur in groups, including contact and conveyance through the senses.

In the centuries following the birth of Tantra, in India, due to the Islamic invasions, the original Red Tantra was officially suppressed and forced to become an occult school. Thus was born the White Tantra, which had monastic aspects and was devoid of sexual intercourse; it was generally more tolerated but gradually lost its identity and merged with Yoga. Today we know it as Tantra Yoga, and it has completely lost its peculiarity of concrete approach to sexuality, typical of the original Tantra.

In practice, White Tantra is a Red Tantra but censored by all those practices that moralists could understand as disreputable. Today White Tantra, which is therefore a mystification of the original Tantra, is used in the West for commercial purposes. Almost all Tantra schools practice White Tantra and therefore do not really teach Tantra.

True Tantra is the Way of reconnecting with one's Self. It is the Way; the Way of the discovery of our genotypical sexual energies that are manifested through the knowledge and practice of the Tantra of Origin.

How it arrived in the West
At the same time with the sexual liberation of the 60s and 70s and the emancipation of women, some students and philosophers began to talk about Tantra and trying to make it a practice approachable even in the West, they made the rituals more agile and less blocking in the calculation of breathing and holding positions. Nowadays, emancipation allows women to get closer to the sexual world, although in Western society it is still believed that sex is more masculine than feminine and the cultural heritage does not allow women to focus on the fact that Tantra is a vehicle to achieve well-being and a higher spirituality.

In the West today Tantra aims to draw two maps, one that shows how to make the sexual experience spiritual and how to unite the earth to the sky, in a terrain where separation and judgment fade away and another map that brings us closer to the unknown sexual world (understood as unconditional love). A world, the Western world, where because of the Catholic religion and the like, there are no schools and traditions and everything is to be invented and experienced. In the West the sexual sphere is a world crushed for two millennia, by taboos and religions that often finds its only expression in private clubs or porn sites.

Tantra with all its erotic experiences is nothing more than a tool that opens physical, emotional and energetic internal spaces and opens to awareness.

Tantra is therefore only the Red Tantra. It is the EIA of liberation that opens to the true expression of one's Self and allows one to escape, both in the

47

imaginary and in the real, from the dimension of the matrix in which sexual energy is mechanically channeled for improper purposes.

The idea of sex is what settled in the imaginary during education, stories and commercial pornography; a program therefore, but so ingrained that individuals believe that it is precisely that pre-programmed way that sexual energy should be expressed. A program that is then gradually enhanced with repetitive experiences that are added together as memories.

The vital energy, or commonly known as sexual energy, is instead what is really the essence of man at its origin; it is what we carry in our genes, but because of the education received in the matrix, is then expressed in fact in an unnatural way.

The matrix has selected over time, with the help of religious morality, a sexual mode completely aimed at procreation ... so mechanical and centered on penetration and orgasm as a goal to be achieved, as if all the wonder of the contact between bodies should be enclosed in an act of a few minutes, between the two genitals. Many people believe they are free sexually because they make much of that mechanical sex, while in reality they are just more slaves; slaves to a trap in which true sexual energy is humiliated and crushed.

The true expression of sexual energy and every moment we love something, a flower, a sunset or a caress. And when that energy expresses itself free from the mechanisms inculcated in the mind, it becomes rite, celebration, connection of bodies, transcendence, healing energy, non-verbal communication, openness to trust between souls, breaking mechanical patterns, projection into the real and the imaginary of a world made of love. Because love cannot be sought... love is a fruit of the tree of freedom. It is therefore freedom that generates love and it is precisely by freeing oneself from the schemes that one encounters love.

Tantra & The Meaning Of Tantric Sex

The word tantra has a precise meaning: technique. It was born as a tantric philosophy of love that brings fullness and intimacy in a relationship through the use of specific sexual techniques. Tantra - also known as sex yoga - is above all love and a new way of seeing life. Tantra is sacred sex because man is the earthly manifestation of a God (Shiva) and woman of a Goddess (Shakti). During sex the woman - who is the active one of the two (you are warned) - must transfer her "cold energy" to the man who transforms it into "hot energy". The purpose of tantric practices is not to reach the couple's orgasm immediately, but to achieve sexual ecstasy for as long as desired. Cool to say, a little harder to get it.It seems that tantrika, historically, although Tantra had not identified the other matrix, the living one, is a representation adherent to that of the Essence of the Original Free Man.

The Tantra of Origin provides nothing but elementary conditioning, morality and prohibitions (i.e. the grid of the individual matrix-slave) from one's own mind, in order to bring out the Self. The following points should therefore be understood, exclusively, in what remains after eliminating this matrix from one's mind, nothing else. Thus, the void created by the cleansing of the antimatrix becomes the emptiness-full.

The tantrika does not live nor does the couple, together with the materialism of the superfluous, as the primary factor of the matrix-slave that disconnects the individual from unconditional universal love, to bring him into the conditioned one, in which the double-matrix operates. He is therefore aware that in "normal" life love does not exist, because calling love the conditional Love is only a euphemism.

1) FREEDOM FROM EXPECTATIONS:

Meaning lack of a foreshadowing of what has to happen and therefore freedom from disappointment when what you wanted does not come true. So tantrika has its own center of gravity that is not dependent on the outside and is not affected by the failure of something or its transformation into something else. Ability then to let go without dwelling on the negative and allow it to alter the soul. The tantrika lives in the HERE AND NOW.

2) FREEDOM FROM SENTIMENTALITY:

Meaning the absence of slipping into pietism and the condescension of religiosity. The tantric way requires a centrality and an ability to observe clearly if one cheats with oneself.

3) FREEDOM FROM THE CONCEPT OF SIN:

Meaning not taking into account the judgment of others because on tantrika have not taken into account the appreciation of the society in which he lives (whether positive or negative appreciation) and therefore much less the moral concepts.

4) FREEDOM FROM FEAR:

understood as the ability 'to overcome both physical and psychological fears that do not advance us on our inner journey and that can become disabling and restrictive for ourselves.

5) FREEDOM FROM DISGUST:

understood as the possibility not to be bound in practice and life by insuperable sensations that prevent us from having an experience, experience being a fundamental aspect of tantric knowledge.

6) FREEDOM FROM THE FAMILY:

Conceived as freedom from family ties and beliefs and from the wrapping mechanisms of the family of origin and ultimately in the ability to distance themselves from the familiar clichés that tend to control and manipulate the other.

7) FREEDOM OF ORIGIN:

Meaning freedom and the possibility of being above all differences in race, skin color, origin and origin. The one who wants to produce the fire does not care which tree the wood he finds belongs to.

8) FREEDOM TO THE INTERDICTIONS:

Understanding as moral constraints or social conformism and therefore freeing the will 'from all laws and ability' to distance themselves from them so as to break the chains of the schemes.

9) FREEDOM FROM THE COUPLE AND MONOGAMY:

Meaning freedom to express the genotype, since monogamy and the couple are not in the nature of man who, like 97% of mammals, has oxytocinic mechanisms that make him genotypically polygamous.

"Free souls vibrate and create the melodies of the cosmos. Sometimes their music touches each other, in moments of symphonies that attract dancing, unique pearls of a universe that plays with forms". Cit. Almalibre Rebelde

10) FREEDOM FROM RELIGIOUS AND POLITICAL SLAVE-MATRIX:

Understood as freedom to be in the genotypical human space-time variant of the here and now; a dimension in which neither dogmas nor social can exist.

11) FREEDOM TO LIVE IN THE DIMENSION OF UNCONDITIONAL UNIVERSAL LOVE.

It is understood as the awareness that love is not a point of arrival and that it cannot be searched for, because this dimension, that of unconditional universal love, is revealed after the liberation of the self, from the matrix-slaughterer's hood. Unconditional universal love is therefore a dimension fruit of self-liberation.

The 3 Golden Rules for Tantric Sex

What are the rules to make the best tantric sex and enjoy its full benefits? First of all, we must say that this is recommended only to people who are already united by a particular relationship. It is not good, therefore, for one-time relationships, but it is much better to put it in a couple context. The affinities will be greater, precisely because it serves to improve all the problems that are the basis of a relationship.

Another rule to enjoy tantric sex is not to be in a hurry. This type of sexuality is in fact, very different from what we all know that, lately, is rather dominated by the cold. Here you can dedicate yourself to your sexuality calmly. This is the only way to achieve total enjoyment. Tantric sex allows you to invigorate the body and make it stronger and more energetic. The atmosphere is very important to carry it out. Yes, therefore, to pillows, special lights, drinks and flowers, to make the environment more welcoming. In fact, it is necessary to relax completely in order to carry it out and to have an intense and lasting pleasure.

First, two people sit opposite each other. You go to connect your breath with the other person first. It sounds like a strange practice but in reality, once you try it, it can really turn into something pleasant. Tantric sex is not something related only to heterosexuality. It is a discipline that also opens to homosexuality and, therefore, even people of the same sex can practice sensual erotic massages to their partner.

It is also true in fact, that homosexuality in the East has never been a taboo, contrary to what often happens in the West. There are many VIPs who have claimed to perform tantric sex. Among them stands out the singer Sting who, years ago, revealed that through this practice, he manages to make sex last for several hours, even continuously.

First of all it is necessary to know your body well, before approaching this philosophy of oriental origin. This happens in the acquisition of awareness of our muscles, but also bones and nerves. Not only about pleasure centers, but about the whole body. Awareness then, must be extended to thoughts and actions. One must pay attention and train concentration. Another suggestion comes from movements, which can be done either alone or in pairs. There are in fact, movements that help in the synchronization of gestures. You should not decide a priori the positions of tantric sex, because otherwise it would lose all its meaning.

Tantra is in fact, something sacred and a freedom of movement. Through a reciprocal massage we can help in the process of knowledge: a massage oil, therefore, can be the only accessory that can serve in tantric sex. Thanks to it you can also get the so-called valley orgasm. What does it consist of? It is a sense of bliss that comes from the degree of intimacy achieved with the partner and not through the mere sexual act.

Since tantra is mutual pleasure, there should be no inhibitions. In this regard, you can also use your voice, if you want. Nothing to do with dirty talking. You talk with whispers, you let your voice flow, you let yourself go in sounds that can be pleasant. Finally, you have to consider that a fundamental role is played by breathing. This should be synchronized as much as possible, in the most natural way. In this way, for example through an embrace, you can exactly perceive your partner's movement and breath and adjust accordingly.

Tantra is something that has nothing to do with selfishness and offers no room for absence. This is all we need to know about the oriental sexual practice of tantric sex, which we have seen have millennial origins. In the West there are some variants of tantric sex, although they are not exactly identical. The real tantra belongs to the East and is no longer even what is practiced today, but what was once done.

TANTRIC SEX CONCEPTS

Many people wonder if tantric sex really works. To make it an intensely erotic moment within the couple you need to follow a series of "tricks". First of all it is necessary to focus on your body and the rhythm of movement, so as to promote the circulation of energy. Voice emissions should not be blocked or inhibited for any reason. In tantric sex you should feel free to express 100% of your pleasure. Finally, breathing deeply also helps to achieve pleasure.

To improve results, there are exercises to be performed together with your partner to improve the whole sphere of sexual affectivity. For example, you can learn to breathe the right way using your diaphragm. You have to breathe in counting to six, hold your breath for another six seconds and exhale for another six. In addition, women must understand where the perineal area is, it can be used to stimulate orgasm only with the pelvic muscles, without any sudden movement. The key to making tantric sex work is to listen to your body, reviewing its different parts and related sensations.

It starts from the first attitude to put into practice or listening: you have to feel and become aware of every inch of your body, understand what gives you pleasure and then get in touch with your emotions at an intimate level never experienced before. You have to get rid of all the stress of everyday life but also of all those limitations that prevent you from letting go, such as low self-esteem and dislike on a physical level. It can help to create before making love a relaxing situation, with candles, soft lights, a massage with scented oil, in short, what you like best.

There are also some tantric exercises to learn to go at the same pace as your partner, so as not to think about sex as a sports performance all projected on the final orgasm. If you surrender to your feelings, you can be able to enjoy every single moment without reaching the orgasmic peak (the so-called valley orgasm).

Fundamental is also the use of the voice, which frees the chest and the pelvis: don't keep the sounds inside you, let them out because they allow you to open your mind.

But the most important aspect of tantra is the relationship between breathing and sexuality: to make love well, in short, you must also learn to breathe well, deeply, to be able to amplify every feeling.

The 4 Key Principles for Sexual Ecstasy
According to tantra there are 4 keys to overcome the psychophysical limits of pleasure, that are:

• Attention - body awareness,

• movement and rhythm,

• the sound,

• the breath.

It is not about looking for the right partner or situation, but about looking inside yourself and expanding your sexual energy. By opening one door at a time, we can enrich our emotional and sexual life.

But how do we do it? Our body is naturally endowed with the 4 keys to pleasure: you just have to learn how to make them turn the right way, to open access to a new erotic dimension.

The attention or body awareness
The first key to pleasure is attention, understood as body awareness. Using this key means learning to listen to your body, first separately, then together with your partner. In what way?

For example, with this exercise, divided into three moments.

First of all, close your eyes, put on relaxing music and focus on the various parts of the body: feet, legs, pelvis, neck...". Those who have difficulty can make small movements to make contact. Then, try to understand how all the parts of your body are, to feel them.

The second part of the exercise is about emotionality: what emotions, what feelings, what climate is inside me? Where do I feel that feeling or this emotion? What is there, in that point?".

Finally, conclude the exercise by composing some mental visualizations that start from this thought: "if I was on a train and I saw my thoughts passing, what would they be and what would they say about me?

During the sexual intercourse we have to pay attention to our body, to the contact area of our physicality with each other, and to the resulting body sensation. Stay in that feeling, do not follow the thoughts, especially those that begin with "duty" (e.g., I should be more excited, etc.). Rather, ask yourself this question: "what do I feel in my body when I make love?"".

Movement and rhythm
The second key to pleasure is represented by movement and rhythm, and this is what tantra says allows the circle of energy. That is why it is important to move together with your partner, in order to unlock them, especially at the level of the pelvis.

To harmonize your rhythm with that of your partner, you can try cycling exercise: sit against your seat, hold your hands and start cycling. The first step is to learn to move together; then you need to synchronize in order to find a shared rhythm. See how long it takes you to find it, who is leading, who is slowing down, who is struggling to keep up. Finally, try some variations on the theme: while pedaling, make some movements (like arching your back), help you find the rhythm and then vary the pattern. During the intercourse everyone should be able to move in total freedom.

During the exercise, try to put body jazz music in the background, to learn how to move even by yourself, and so to loosen the body first the neck, then the shoulders, progressively descending and prepare it to follow all forms of pleasure.

The sound
The third key to pleasure is the voice, with all its vibrations and sound. The vocal emissions and sounds coming out of the throat, in fact, free the mind, unlock the chest and the belly (pelvis), and therefore the pleasure. Do not hold them back (it is not mandatory to "shout"), let them flow into the body and then out of the throat, naturally: it is self-exciting, and helps to put sexual energies into circulation.

Breathing
The fourth key to pleasure is breathing, which according to tantra, can also be the most devious way to inhibit pleasure and excitement, because if the breath is short or shallow, we do not oxygenate our body well: it is like starting in fourth gear, but with the handbrake pulled.

Learning to breathe well, deeply, therefore, is fundamental, for example with this simple exercise:

The breath must be soft and circular. As you breathe in, count to 6, hold for another 6 and release, always counting up to 6, because the phases of breathing must be symmetrical. If you practice in this way, you begin to change not only your breathing, but also the way you perceive your body. When you are in a couple, then, as for the movements, it is important to synchronize the breath with that of the partner, because this allows all the energy to circulate and amplify the sensations. And also the emotions: according to the oriental philosophy, by taking 3 deep breaths when you embrace a person you love very much, you double your happiness.

Some men might be a bit skeptical to try tantric sex, which proposes a different approach to sexuality from the "western" one. How to convince him? Instead of many speeches, a playful mode that can give immediate pleasure can be useful. For example, starting with a sensual massage, taking time to explore sensoriality. And then, lead him into this new erotic dimension, taking on the role of geisha: be sure that he will rely on your guidance.

To summarize...

Tantra and its techniques are not easy, but neither are impossible. Be careful: tantric practices are for very close couples. They will prove to be an epic fail if they lack great confidence, feeling and desire at the top. Ready to give it a try? There is no need to buy a guide to tantric sex, just start getting involved with the four basic tantric exercises:

• Live the present moment and be aware of your body: listen to your and her body, listen to your breathing, look intensely into each other's eyes, love every detail of each other. There is no space to think about what you have to do next, what commitments you have to fix, what problems at work you have, what physical defects your partner might see. During tantric love you love every detail of yourself and your partner. No mental limit, no physical limit, no prejudice. Kiss each other, touch each other, observe each other all the time in the relationship.

• Rhythm and movement are fundamental: they put energy into circulation and must be done in harmony. You move together, at the same speed, possibly slowly and deeply, especially at the pelvis level. No rush into penetration, please. It must be almost a dance.

• Tantra breathing is a must: how to prolong the pleasure if not by controlling the breath? The more relaxed and softer it is, the more it oxygenates the erogenous zones. The top would be to synchronize your breath with that of your partner: try to inhale counting to six, hold your breath for six seconds and exhale for another six.

• Prolonged coitus: the sensations are so deep that you will naturally postpone your orgasm. It won't have to be your goal, you won't have to chase it, but neither will you have to hold it if you feel it exploding. He doesn't even need a full erection: it is enough that the penis remains inside you to stimulate it with the contraction of the pelvic muscles and continue to feel a super pleasure. It's called valley orgasm and it comes from listening to the sensations: the warmth, the softness of the skin, the scent, the features of your partner and so on.

The Orgasm in Tantric Sex

That orgasm is the crowning achievement of sexual intercourse is something we take for granted. On the contrary, when it is not achieved (constantly), perplexities, crises and finally couple problems begin. Yes, because in Western society, sex has a linear approach: from courtship to the sexual act, which ends with orgasm, possibly both. But not for everyone is so. In Tantric sex, for example, this view fades.

Tantra is a set of doctrines based on the principle of transgression. The transgression was primarily that of the order based on purity.

But Tantrism has always had an objective that goes beyond the simple violation of the rules. Simplifying a lot, one could say that in Tantrism the person questions his own person as he has always understood it. The goal is an overcoming of the subjectivity of the individual, his values and his identity. This process in the Tantric vision leads man in a dimension where he comes into contact with his true self and therefore with the divine dimension.

In the tantric vision of sex, pleasure is not the point of arrival, as some believe. Often, in fact, we hear about intense orgasms and legendary performances. But the matter is much more complex because even sex becomes a means. It is part of a systematic project to get in touch, through pleasure, with one's deep self.

Among the characteristics of tantric sex, as far as men are concerned, there is the practice of semen retention. Orgasm, as we understand it in the West, does not actually happen. This practice produces an accumulation of energy that is not released through ejaculation. In short, man manages to control a process that in the eyes of many is pure abandonment of control. The accumulated energy, often called kundalini, goes up towards the upper part of the body. In this way you reach an ecstatic state that goes far beyond simple physical pleasure.

This state can only be reached thanks to a very complex path that is difficult to achieve in the West. It is not a path for everyone. It requires a solid yogic training, ability to control emotions, ascetic practice and spiritual maturity. It is also necessary to pass through the experience of emptiness, a test not suitable for everyone, which involves advanced meditative skills.

Tantrism is for many people synonymous with freedom, deriving from the abandonment of the rules; it is no coincidence that it began to fascinate the West in '68, a period of great claims in this sense. However, it has often been mystified, made a sort of pass for epic sexual experience.

Yes, because we often think we can use superficially practices from other cultures, as if they were shortcuts for the purposes we set out for (and in fact in the West tantra has also known a light version known as neotantra). It is not a test to do with tantric sex, which is a dangerous operation. It is an extreme way reserved for a few; if you are not ready, it is easy to be a victim. Not everyone, in fact, is prepared to make contact with their own depths and manage the disruptive force of some emotions. "Tantric sex is reserved for the hero, that is to say, the one who is able to bear the liberation of energy that comes from it.

Although not within everyone's reach, this practice retains a remarkable charm, as well as an extremely equal view of the relationship. The ideal tantric union presupposes an equality between man and woman. Both must be aware of the mystical purpose of sexual practice. And both see themselves as divinities: they are the mirror of a divine image of each other. In sexual intercourse they "die", they dissolve, one into the other; as the Persian mystics write, what remains at the end of the union between lover and beloved is only Love.

Pure Bliss: What Is The Valley Orgasm?

Have you ever heard of valley orgasm? At first glance, this expression suggests that it is a dichotomous concept with another: where there is a valley there is also a mountain. And indeed it is so: "mountain orgasm" and "valley orgasm" are in fact concepts related to tantric sex, so let's talk about the spiritual side of sex and sexuality. There is a lot of talk about tantric sex - and many people call it an urban legend, a myth - but tantra is real, even if you need to deepen the discipline - there are also special seminars - and what we are going to tell you is for information purposes only.

One of the ways in which orgasm is usually indicated is "climax", i.e. peak. But that climax is actually the so-called mountain orgasm.

To understand, let's go behind the figurative image: a mountain, drawn as a fixed stereotype, is a large inverted V, in which there is an ascent, a vertex and a descent. In this similarity, the ascent is represented by all those actions that are carried out when having sex - from foreplay, to penetration, to the change of position, and so on. When you get to the top of the mountain, you feel the orgasm of the mountain, but the descent is sweet and pleasant, not fast and immediate. The mountain orgasm does not disappear immediately, but if "cultivated" in the right way, it can allow you to reach the valley orgasm.

Tantric sex can lead to the so-called valley orgasm. It may sound absurd but to achieve it you have to do absolutely nothing. Usually when making love you feel anxiety and tension because the goal is to make a good impression. In this practice of Indian origin, however, you do not have to worry about anything, it is not even necessary that the penis is erect. The intimate contact alone is enough. You need to have the muscles of the body relaxed and, at most, stimulate the male penis by contracting the pelvic muscles. The movements must be very slow and intense. Valley orgasm is a pleasure that comes from listening to simple sensations such as perfume, warmth, softness of the skin, partner's features, it is something that can only be achieved when anxiety, stress and effort are completely forgotten. The result, however, will be particularly intense, almost a form of bliss.

In the article The Art of Loving on Osho's website we read an invitation not to break away after having reached both orgasm: if you don't break away you can reach the valley orgasm, a state of deep well-being and closeness, love and meditation that somehow interpenetrate as the two bodies have interpenetrating just before. But it is possible only through silent observation, just before returning to normal, to the state that precedes coitus. Afterwards there can also be moments of pampering, indeed they are very important, almost essential, perhaps through massages with oils, good music and a little scented candles.

How To Reach The Valley Orgasm?

To reach orgasm in the valley... nothing must be done. Yes, it may seem absurd to you, but in fact all the action has taken place before and the valley orgasm is precisely the speculative and meditative phase of the relationship.

Attention, however: this does not mean that immediately after the relationship you have to put on your clothes or go to sleep, this is precisely what the tantra advises you to avoid. Sex is a sacred moment and must be treated as such. So let's go through the stages of the relationship to better understand how to behave and to make the most of sex as an experience that combines body and soul.

You are in bed - or wherever you like - with your partner or partner. There are the preliminaries and then the actual relationship that may or may not include penetration. The relationship culminates in the upstream orgasm - when and if it arrives - after which you take your time. Remaining close, embraced, in contemplation. The ideal is to reach the climax together, but it is something that can come about through deep mutual knowledge and practice - sometimes even of a sentimental nature, not just distinctly sexual. So after the climax you stay still, enjoy the moment, without being caught unprepared by what is usually called the refractory period and which leads to post-coital sleepiness.

And after that? You may be pervaded by a feeling of well-being that lasts for hours. Because your soul - as well as of course your body - has found fulfillment in what happened between the sheets.

Tantric sex obviously can't be improvised, it requires a physical but above all mental preparation, not doing anything of what one is usually led to do arouses many perplexities in Western culture. Those who practice tantric love define this experience as "cosmic" or "divine", it is a flow of energies that flow from the bodies, away from thoughts, from the pursuit of pleasure and the stress that comes with it. It is no coincidence that Western society has to deal with performance anxieties of all kinds and types, from erection problems to the female ones of never reaching orgasm.

Speaking in technical terms the tantric one is defined "Valley Orgasm" precisely because there is no need to reach the climax of pleasure, this feeling of "arrive - not arrive" is already very pleasant and deep, so that orgasm is really a surplus, an optional.

As we were saying, psychological preparation is essential, one cannot approach tantra if one does not deeply believe in making love as something beyond orgasm, penetration, it is something spiritual and intense that disorientates and leaves one almost interdicted.

TANTRIC SEX TECHNIQUES
Tantric sex aims at the full sharing of emotions, sensations, both physical and mental. It unhinges the voracity typical of modern sexuality, understood as a pure vehicle of carnal pleasure, aimed at achieving a pleasant orgasm. Calmness, slowness and sharing are the basis, instead, of this doctrine that aims, as an objective, the improvement of sexuality, always, as clarified, passing from awareness and sharing of feelings and emotions.

The tantra practices focus, in fact, on the visual attention of the lovers, on tactile sensations, passing through the symbiosis of breath. Movement and rhythm, especially in the part of the pelvis, are the key words of tantric sex, these are what put in circulation a lot of energy, more than what we think we hide inside us, allowing us to unlock them, renewing the pleasure of the senses and the inner one. Tantric sex aims to allow those who practice it to better know both their body and that of their partner, encouraging the harmony of the couple.

The 10 Tantric Sex Positions
Taking new positions can help renew the passion. Before reviewing the best positions of tantric sex, it is necessary to follow some very specific preliminaries in order to achieve full physical and mental satisfaction. In this regard, partners during tantric love must find themselves in a condition of complete relaxation. They must observe and contemplate themselves. Only when this balance will be achieved, only when the outpouring of glances and breaths will be maximum, then and only then you can proceed. Tantra

positions can help you get started the right way. These 4 main positions look like yoga positions for couples and will make you feel fused together:

• Lotus position: the most famous one, made a cult by Sting himself (who told the press that he could have tantric sex for more than 7 hours in a row. Not bad!). Him sitting, her sitting on his thighs wrapping him with her own legs and holding him in a hug while moving rhythmically. Looking into his eyes it's the key.

• Variant of the lotus position: sitting facing each other, legs intertwined to merge into the penetration.

• Position of the hot chair: him sitting on the chair and leaning against the backrest, her sitting on him with her legs leaning against his shoulders.

• Variant of the position of the hot chair: both kneeling, he behind her pushing from behind while she makes circular movements with her pelvis. Super hot.

Lotus Position
Perhaps the best known among the tantric sexual positions to be exploited in bed is that lotus flower where the man stands cross-legged with the woman on top of him, crossing his thighs behind his partner's back to wrap him and look him intensely in the eyes.

Lotus Variant
This basic tantric position can have several variations, such as the one where man and woman are sitting opposite each other and the legs intertwine almost as if to create a unique being perfectly fused together.

Ground Position
The typical position with him sitting and her on top of him is great to try even lying on the floor, or with pillows to make the intercourse more comfortable.

Tantric Positions With Chair
The most acrobatic lovers, who want to try new tantric positions, can also achieve pleasure with the help of a chair, where the seated man can welcome the woman who puts her legs over her partner's shoulders.

Crouching
Among the best tantric sexual positions to try with a chair is also the one in which the woman is squatting over the man resting her feet on the edge.

The Bomb

The tantric position of the bomb involves the man sitting on a chair and the woman on top of him, without touching the ground with her feet.

Tantric Positions In Water

Tantra can also be safely put into practice in water, for example on a swimming pool, with the man sitting on the ladder and the woman crouched over him.

Tantric Position In Bathtub

If you have a bathtub, you can try the classic tantric sexual position with hot water as an additional sexy and relaxing ingredient.

Tantric sex is the key to open the doors of pleasure, release sexual energy, allowing you to experience special sensations while experiencing very long intercourse times. This discipline of oriental origins changes the approach to sex, which is declined as a tool to achieve harmony of the senses, harmony of the couple, inner and outer balance, all passing from a unique and extremely captivating sensory experience.

The Tantric Massage: What Is It & How To Do It

Tantric massage is an ancient Indian practice that promotes the understanding of oneself and others by light and circular touches, leading to a feeling of well-being that is both union and liberation: let's look at all the benefits.

Through tantric masasggio and stimulation of certain energy points of the figure.
It provides a tremendous deal of sensory pleasure as well as an improvement in self-perception and self-esteem to the individual who receives it. That is good to increase the knowledge and harmony of the couple. Tantric massage is based on ancient Indian teachings, which in turn date back to texts of pre-vedic cultures, the origin of which is still quite mysterious and controversial. The ancient population of the Harappa, for example, put significant attention to tantra's energy, particularly the female form and its element, water; in the middle of their homes, there was a large swimming pool and a room with a large bed on which to conduct tantric massage.

How To Do The Tantric Massage

The tantric massage is structured in three phases.

> In the first phase we focus on meditation and meditation, creating in a suitable and intimate place, such as the bedroom, a cozy environment, with soft lighting, incense, practicing breathing exercises and reciting mantras.

> The second phase is focused on slow, circular and light massages on face and body, from legs to arms, passing through the pelvic area, back, neck and head, with gentle touches along the vital energy channels, chakras and nadi. A warm and delicate vector oil, such as coconut oil, is used.

> The last phase is relaxation: sipping a warm herbal tea you share the experience with those who have practiced it, verbalizing what you have experienced. Advantages of tantric massage.

All The Benefits Of Tantric Massage

Everyone can enjoy advantages and benefits, including a new experience of sexuality, not limited in space and time, but perceived as omnipresent energy to be channeled into every cell of the body. In this way, anxiety, stress concerns are dissolved, along with other tensions.

Far from being a sexual practice, tantric massage acts on the genitals by dissolving blockages and going to relax the first chakra, using Tantra lingam techniques for men and Tantra yoni for women. There is also the technique of Tantra Kundalini massage. Tantric massage, a practice aiming at rediscovering the sanctity of the body as an element and physical envelope of the soul, combines personal growth and sensory experiences targeted at well-being.

Tantra Kundalini Massage

This is one of the most curious, fascinating and sensual forms of tantra massage: we are talking about the Kundalini technique, which ideally represents a snake, which in turn symbolizes the primordial energies that reside in each of us, to be precise at the first chakra. The snake is the metaphor of transformation, in reference to its peculiarity of losing and rebuilding the skin regularly, and the transformation is associated with well-being in physical and spiritual terms as well as enlightenment (remember that the tantra philosophy aims at the elevation of the individual).

The Kundalini tantric massage, in particular, awakens the primordial energy of the first chakra - located in the perineal area - the starting point for a tantra massage that also involves the genital areas, without excluding any part of the body, until reaching the seventh chakra, the top of the neck.

During the Kundalini tantra massage the chakras should be progressively purified, so that the Kundalini - i.e. primordial energy - can get the upper hand by breaking down obstacles such as attachment to physical and material pleasure (this is linked to sexual intercourse seen as an act of donation not necessarily aimed at orgasm), as well as to our ego. At the moment of

Kundalini's awakening, in the recipient of this specific tantra massage, thanks to the harmonious and enveloping movements with which it is massaged, the entire body will experience a feeling of complete well-being and total pleasure.

The effectiveness of the massage can be achieved thanks to very prolonged manipulations (even two hours) performed by an experienced operator: do not try this massage without mastering the technique perfectly. The purpose of the massage is to promote relaxation of the muscles adjacent to the spine, to prepare the central channel (sushumua) to welcome the upward flow of kundalini energy. Once the back, shoulders and neck are open, the lower back, including legs, feet and buttocks, must be massaged vigorously to release tension in the lower extremities to facilitate kundalini upward flow.

With the back of the body relaxed, the lower pelvic area is prepared to be relaxed and opened through a circular deep massage into the sacral and pelvic area. In this way the main natii or astral canal is purified so that the kundalini currents can flow and join the Vishnu. The direction is always from bottom to top. For this reason, the work on the body starts at the bottom. The chakra centers are opened and balanced in order, from the bottom, then from the muladhara chakra, to the other, through the other chakra centers to the sahasrara. This opening serves to prepare the body for further releases and movements of kundalini energy.

When the lower pelvic cavity begins to open thanks to deep massage, the upper chakra siri must be prepared with gentle touches along the thorn in the direction of the neck. The highest chakra, ajna, and the Sahasrara area at the top of the head, are prepared for the opening through an energetic balance obtained without contact with the body. The opening of the subsequent chakras will create a passage that will allow the kundalini to radiate upwards. This first part of the massage, in which the recipient is lying face down, is preparatory to the second part, in which he will be lying on his back.

Once the chakra centers are activated, the kundalini energy contained in the muldhara chakra, placed at the base of the column, is gently released. The kundalini energy is often called "snake energy" because it lies inert, coiled at the base of the vertebral axis; it is static and sealed at the root of the spine, just beyond the tip of the sacrum. Releasing this energy creates two forces, one centripetal (Shakti) and the other centrifugal (Shiva). Shakti is directed upward to the highest chakras, to complete a union with Shiva. whose original source, according to Tantra, is the sun. It is thanks to the union of these two forces that harmony and balance are achieved, according to ancient Tantric beliefs.

Often the first experience of releasing kundalini energy is disappointing: the energy hardly rises above the first or second chakra. However, after a number of sessions that varies from subject to subject, the release of "awakened" kundalini energy takes place: those who have experienced it describe it as an unforgettable experience, in which one perceives a sort of liquid fire flowing up the sushumna, through the head and the top of the body.

MULTIPLE ORGASM

The orgasm isn't the cherry on top for many people when it comes to lovemaking. It's the entire sundae. They treat foreplay and intercourse as if there were playing poker, and if they play their cards right, they win the pot and cash those chips in for a mind-blowing, body quivering orgasm.

What if they don't climax? Well, then they treat the whole experience as though they won the pot only to discover the chips can't be cashed in. They're stuck with two handfuls of cheap plastic. Everyone can agree that orgasms feel amazing. It's a sure sign that all the elements in lovemaking came together correctly to give that partner a moment of ecstasy.

As great as they are, it's a huge mistake to make that the goal of lovemaking, especially when practicing the Kama Sutra. When practicing the techniques, the experience shouldn't judge whether or not one or both partners experienced orgasms. They shouldn't even be basing it on how close they came to climaxing. Orgasms can be very elusive, especially for women. Sometimes thinking about it makes it difficult actually to have it. Sometimes, it doesn't happen because it just didn't happen.

Male Orgasm Basics

The male orgasm is something that most people have witnessed or seen if they have ever watched porn or heard about it in the media. The male orgasm is made to be extremely simple and easy to achieve, but in this part, we will examine it in more detail and break it down into more specific pieces.

To start, are you aware that there are different types of male orgasms? You are probably aware of this if you are a male, but you may not be a female. The term male orgasm includes any and every type of orgasm that involves the male's genitals.

Orgasm and Ejaculation

Ejaculation and orgasm for males are two different events, even though they most often happen simultaneously. This fact makes them often misunderstood, as many think that ejaculation is a sign of orgasm. If orgasm occurs and ejaculation co-occurs, this is called an ejaculatory orgasm.

There is another type of orgasm that happens when ejaculation does not. As you likely guessed, this type is called a non-ejaculatory orgasm. That is sometimes called dry orgasm, which is also very typical. A man can achieve orgasm without ejaculation, which counts as an orgasm.

How to Stimulate the Prostate to Achieve Orgasm
Once you have found the prostate, you can massage this area and let the sensations build gently. Keep going like this and determine what type of movements or pressure feels best. As you continue to stimulate it, let the pleasure make to the point of orgasm. When you are comfortable with this spot, try having your partner encourage it for you. Having someone else's hands touch it for you will feel different than your own, and with your free hand, you can turn yourself and your partner on in other ways.

The prostate is sometimes referred to as the male G-Spot. It has many similar properties to the female G-Spot, such as how you can find it and how it needs t to be stimulated to reach orgasm.

Female Orgasm Basics
To make a woman orgasm, you will need to know and understand the female body, including all places where, when stimulated, a woman will feel pleasure and maybe even orgasm. Both sexes can learn more about the female body, whether you are a female or a male with a female partner.

How to Stimulate the Clitoris to Achieve Orgasm
Once you have found the clitoris, you will stimulate it to achieve orgasm. Begin by gently placing two fingers on it and putting a bit of pressure. Rub it by moving your fingers in small circles-making sure to be gentle. Continue to do this, and she should begin to get more aroused the more you do this. By rubbing the clitoris, you will be able to stimulate the entire clitoris, even the part that you cannot see, which will cause the woman to start to become wet in her vaginal area for her body to prepare for sex.

How to Stimulate the G-Spot to Achieve Orgasm
To give a woman pleasure by stimulating her G-Spot, you will need to press on it repeatedly until she reaches orgasm. That can be done using your fingers, a penis, or sex toys of various sorts. The G-Spot needs to receive continued and consistent stimulation for the pleasure to build enough for her to reach orgasm.

Since a woman can have two different types of orgasms, one from stimulating the clitoris and a different one from penetration or hitting the G-spot, this could be why a woman can reach orgasm during oral sex, or by having her clitoris stimulated but has trouble getting the same level of pleasure during penetrative sex. In many positions, the G-spot is not produced by the man's penis, resulting in the woman having some fun but not enough to reach orgasm. For a great experience as a couple, knowing what makes the woman feel great is paramount.

SEX GAMES

- Honey, why don't we try something new tonight?
- Darling, at most, you change the color of the sheets and open a bottle of sparkling wine!

Okay, she didn't say no, and that's a good start.

But not even that veiled, our little creative streak comes out under the blankets. If you're a man who wants to make his partner happy or a woman who feels she has to take over the situation for the sake of the couple, you'll probably want some suggestions or even just a different point of view.

There are several little things you can do to add spice to the sexual act, without having to have special needs or risk your health. Obviously, when we talk about "putting pepper" we are not literally referring to a "spicy genital" (which would take you directly to the hospital), but to increase the complicity and, therefore, the enjoyment.

Erotic games are a fun way to impress your partner but also to revive and consolidate your love story. For this reason, we wanted to take a closer look to this topic by focusing on several aspects: we started from erotic games for women and men, such as role-playing to deepen games with rules to be established, to the more greedy ones, which involve the use of food, or cards.

We didn't stop here: there are many games for the couple, which you can do by choosing the right dildo, and, also, we have selected the most beautiful erotic games to download on your smartphone. So many ideas that we do not want to reveal immediately but that you will find in the chapter. What did you want more?

If your sex life is no longer as satisfying as it used to be, perhaps because of everyday life and routine, don't worry: with a good dose of imagination, you can live torrid and passionate (and extremely funny) moments in no time. Here are some ideas:

1. Choose the perfect erotic game for you and prepare the screenplay
Whatever your choice, for an erotic game with flakes you can enrich the screenplay with details. Also, knowing the role you are going to "play" can give you even more confidence and make it more intriguing. Black bows, masks, costumes, lights, everything will help to make your evening really hot!
2. If you have not time to organize a sex game...improvise!
Depending on your preferences, you could also simply decide the plot of the sexual role-playing game, without too many frills, and then let yourself go to improvisation, acting and reacting according to the development of the situation. If you feel awkward at first, don't worry, with practice you will gain confidence and feel free.

3. Think before you act: erotic games yes, uncomfortable situations no!

Try to predict what you really don't want to happen. It's a game and as a game, it's meant to entertain you. So say no to situations or actions that may make you feel uncomfortable and don't do anything you don't feel able to do. And if you realise that the situation is uncomfortable, just say no, it's simple.

4. How to choose the game to play? Make compromises

What erotic game to choose? Obviously one we both like. It's not necessarily an easy choice, because erotic fantasies vary greatly from person to person. Try to find a compromise that combines both ideas, or, alternately, try to meet as much as possible. That's what love is, isn't it?

5. Take your partner's wishes into account

Even the small details count. Some things may seem small to you that are important to the other person. An example? If he or she tells you that absolutely wants you to put on a red lipstick, don't argue about how, or why, take a red lipstick and make him or her happy. It's all part of his fantasy, isn't it? If he asks you to wear a monkey suit, you have our full support that you're a little perplexed...

6. Think about accessories, they can make a difference during an erotic role-playing game.

Lingerie, lace, garters, corsets. Or loose shirts, unusual clothes, hats, masks. Why not think big? If you prefer simplicity, opt only for the "screenplay", in some cases words are enough, the description of a different situation, pretending who you are not, who you would like to be in that moment. What matters most in these cases is imagination!

Role Playing Games

Erotic role-playing games can be a fun pastime for a couple. Let's say couple for some reasons: some of these roleplays require a good dose of trust between the parties and also their function can be to rekindle the flame of passion.

Role playing in bed is the same as impersonating a character, as if you were acting. Of course, the characters may be a bit parodied - even between the sheets some laughter never hurts and creates a bond in the couple - and maybe something could go wrong. You have to remember that you have to act safely: in other words, if you're dressed as Batman or Batgirl, maybe you shouldn't jump from the dresser to the bed. The other important thing is to remember that everything is allowed in sex, as long as you agree and there is consensuality.

Erotic Role Playing Games: Why try them?

Actually, the more correct question is: why not? We mentioned earlier that erotic role-playing games can help you get out of the routine. If you've been together for many years, the problem may not be indifferent: as time goes by, the demands of everyday life become more and more pressing, the desire may diminish. It happens, it's nobody's fault, but you can always run for cover.

Another point in favour of roleplaying lies precisely in the trust that must be established between the people involved: for example, in some of the games that we will describe, an unprofessional bondage could be envisaged - so don't exaggerate, those who practice BDSM even take courses so that their practices are inoffensive - and this can only happen in a relaxed atmosphere of complete trust.

The gardener

The scenario.

He, a gardener hired to fix the plants in your house, rings the intercom. You, after the shower, wrapped in a silk kimono, go and open the door. You introduce yourself, you start talking, the erotic tension that caresses you like the summer breeze. He starts to work and you watch him, while his muscles move flickering under your t-shirt. The longer you wait, the more the electricity between you will be palpable and the desire will increase.

The theme.

This fantasy is that of the unexpected encounter, which you didn't think could happen. You like me, I like you: there's no point in going around it. We already know how it will end. Often this is the role-playing game that gives the most satisfaction, if properly organized and if not run too fast.

To vary

It doesn't have to be a gardener: you can opt for a plumber, a satellite technician, an electrician... in short, you can choose! Why not, he could just be the new neighbour who comes to ask if you have sugar...

The Hitchhiker

The scenario

You can decide to develop this script even using a car, as long as you have a not too busy and isolated place to stop. The only obligation for you is to wear a skirt (easier for when the time comes x...) and, in case you are in a real location and not recreated at home, you will be even more discreet.

The theme

The promiscuity, the risk of being discovered at any moment, but also the fleeting sex, the one that makes you pump adrenaline into your bloodstream. What's more, being in a place as small as a machine facilitates the growth of desire.

To vary

Choose if you prefer him to take the first step or if you prefer to play the enterprising woman who is not afraid to take what she wants, in this case the charming man behind the wheel who was kind enough to give you a lift...

Back to School

The scenario

The most classic of couple's erotic games. The professor and the student. Him stopping you to ask you something about your studies, or why you weren't paying attention in class and... and one thing leads to another... the fatal attraction kicks in and you can't keep your hands off each other.

The Theme

It is one of the fantasies that both men and women can share: it often happens that the student becomes obsessed with their teacher.

To vary

In addition to change the type of subject taught from time to time, you can also reverse the roles and be the teacher. Again, consider whether to be enterprising and "plagiarize" your student or whether you prefer the opposite to happen!

The Servant

The scenario

One of them will play the servant. He who cannot make decisions unless his master defines them. It will be the latter who will hold the reins of the game and will be able to decide what to say or do to his submissive, who will not take any initiative but will be content to carry out orders without breathing a word.

The theme

Total obedience. As well as seeing your every wish come true, whether it is a sensual back massage or satisfying your desire for a simple orange juice.

To vary

Dominatrix and slave, queen and servant. They can change roles and locations, but the fantasy remains the same. Choose if you prefer to give the orders or if you prefer to execute them.

The Spy

Here you can also go into BDSm - remember to agree on a safe word if you go too far. One of the two components of the couple decides to interpret the international criminal and the other the CIA or KGB spy - perhaps adapting the accent according to the choice. Whoever interprets the criminal can be bound and be directed to the truth through small sexual concessions or particular stimulations. It remains obvious that everything must be consensual.

Once Upon a Time

Curious to experience old-fashioned romantic love? Then the role-playing game presupposes a script set in an ad hoc residence, maybe a castle and a dress code and strictly vintage beauty style. The important thing is to leave ample space for courtship and listen to body language without hurry to get to the point.

The Strangers

Does sex fantasies include sex with strangers? Maybe dogging? In this case the role-playing game that suits you catapults you among people, in the role of two strangers (especially not immediately) end up in each other's arms. For the location don't put brakes on your imagination: from the lobby of a hotel (where you can then book a room) to a concert (where you'll be forced to look for yourself in the crowd), passing through the airport (maybe with a final surprise and unexpected romantic weekend) it's worth everything.

The Porn Movie

Among the most chosen roleplay situations are those inspired by the plots of erotic films. Often these plots are quite anti-feminist - these movies are mostly directed at men - so you won't find female plumbers coming to fix a certain pipe - even though we think it's a plausible way in the roleplay you'll choose, even more realistic from anatomical similarity.

Like the plumber, you can get a visit from the electrician, the chimney sweep even if you don't have a chimney, the TV technician and so on. Of course, such roles are not only the prerogative of the man, but can be played by the woman, according to your preferences.

Hot Ideas To Try At Least Once In a Lifetime

The Mirror

Mirror, mirror of my cravings, who are the most sensual of all the kingdoms? Placing a mirror by your bedside will help you capture every moment of your relationship. Especially during the "little train", you would never want to miss the expression of your partner during orgasm...

Come Here And Now

In a dressing room, in the disco bathroom... It's fun to experience the thrill of a quickie. Which, by the way, helps to stay faithful: The Journal of Sex Research claims that 67% of people cheat just for the taste of the forbidden. And the 'quickie' has all the ingredients to give the same feeling, but without unnecessary guilt.

Shoes Up

54% of men find it very exciting if you don't take your heels off in bed. Why limit yourself to those? Not taking your clothes off is a trick to give sex what a man will take as a compliment to his manhood...

Stop-And-Go

The principle can be applied to intercourse: when you're about to come, you stop (or slow down) for a minute, then you recover. Some research argues that orgasm can become as much as 40% more intense.

Remote Vibrator

You're at dinner, for instance. You brought your vibrator, which is activated by remote control. You brought your finger to click. There's nothing better than getting excited in public. The appetizer of your romantic dinner could be just that.

Double mint

To enrich oral sex, just make some mint tea and take a few sips before "getting to work". The contrast between the warmth of the drink and the stimulating effect of mint will be an unexpectedly pleasant variable for both of you.

Slow Sex

Sometimes, however, it's slowness that gains points for an intercourse. Just do "the usual", but at a speed four times slower. Both partners will have more time to create an energetic and emotional bond, as well as physical, and the orgasm will also become more intense and profound.

Open

If exists one thing that will make you remember sexual intercourse forever, it is to do it in a public place. Whether it's a park, a sparsely populated alleyway or the sushi bar bathroom, the idea of being discovered makes a quickie something magical.

The Latex

The latex tracksuit. It's a bit S&M, but it's undoubtedly effective, especially with strategic openings that allow the ordinary course of the act. Just try the latex underwear.

Briefs in the drawer

"Going commando", as the British say, is not only the passion of stars like Britney Spears or Lindsay Lohan, paparazzied without briefs in embarrassing out of the car, but it's the best way to tell a man we like him. At dinner, all you have to do is guide his hand under the table and let him sense the "surprise".

Ciak, Action!

You have to put the camera on the bedside table, press Rec and start the hormones.You don't need to see the shot again, what makes everything exciting is just the thought that the camera is filming you.

The Sex Compilation

Doing it in music time can be a unique detonator. The orgasm can be much more intense if caused by different "gaits". So, start a playlist in "random" mode and let the mood of the song guide you.

Furniture

Very exciting, both for him and her, is to be literally banged up on a choice of house furniture. In front of the mirror while he's buttoning his shirt, or on the coffee table in the lobby while she's looking for her car keys.
You say I forgot the washing machine while spinning?

The Magic Balls

Ancient oriental practice, with a lanyard with balls that rotate. They usually rub the intimate areas of the woman, increasing her perceptions and pleasure.

I Finished The Laundry

This thing will literally drive your man insane. Just let him see from under the table that you don't have any panties... Waiter, check, please!

The Route Of The Gorge

Sprinkle yourselves with sweet and delicious things. Each erogenous zone of the body can be associated with a food you particularly love, such as honey, chocolate, cream... the rest will be a slow, caloric walk to pleasure. After all, there's no doubt that you'll be able to dispose of the calories you've acquired in a short while.

Look At Me!

One study reveals that 72% of men get excited by the vision of a woman who gives herself pleasure. So why not put on a private show where you masturbate while he watches you?

Striptease Of Balloons

You're dressed, or rather, you're naked but covered in balloons. All you need is a needle and a lot of attention. Can you pierce them all before you jump on them?

The Lubricant

The perfect lover's kit accessory. There are also edible versions, to give free rein to the most intense and tasty pleasure. Or even just for situations where you are in a hurry to get started and your body fluids are not responding.

The Film

Years pass, generations change, but the pleasure of being filmed or observed is a natural stimulant. We are so "voyeurs" that we would like to experience the same situation even as observers. Do you have a bedside table and a small camera?

At Parents' Home

Yes, I know, it's always part of the "what if they catch us?" package, but you'll admit that mom and dad's bed, or the stairs in the family's wine cellar on your way to get the wine, have their own charm.

The Vortex

Have you ever been overwhelmed by the real whirlwind of emotions? A web of bodies and souls that becomes one with the soft lights of the room. Weave a sheet, tie one end to the bed and the other to the woman's wrists. After lying under her, give vent to your thoughts among the shadows of the woman's slowly descending body. Let yourself be overwhelmed by the vortex of heat of the two bodies meeting.

SEX TOYS

Introductions

More and more couples are relying on sex toys to increase pleasure and erotic intrigue. But even erotic games have their golden rules.Until not so long ago, sex toys and sex games were still a taboo subject. Or, at least, it wasn't talked about so openly. Today, however, we are faced with a real sex toy aesthetic that even becomes a design object to show off.

According to a recent survey conducted by LoveLab (a company that deals with "cosmetics for couples"), as many as 6 out of 10 Americans have used or use sex toys with a peak in the age range from 30 to 45 years. But that's not all, according to this survey women are the most passionate fans of these objects. So much so that there is talk of a real widespread phenomenon: Sex Fun.

A fun and conscious transgression

If for a long time sex toys have been sold (and bought) almost secretly, today they come out with all their fun and mischief. But this is no longer a transgression of a few: by now erotic toys have been cleared through customs as an exceptional resource and have become bed-friends of many couples.

It's mainly women who love sex toys and, again according to the data collected by LoveLab, the female public is also aware of this type of purchase (just like it's happening for cosmetics). Women's favorite sex toys are, in fact, natural, vegan and not tested on animals. Later in this chapter we will make a list of the best sex toys and a guide to choose which one to buy according to your needs.

But why all this love for sex toys and couple cosmetics? First of all, because fortunately there is a growing conviction that satisfying sexuality is everyone's right and that the achievement of pleasure is a matter of complicity rather than performance.

No to performance anxiety
Thus, the sexual pleasure and sexuality of the couple become a much broader issue than sexual performance and penetration. And, in this kind of more "democratic" context, it is also legitimate to resort to aids such as sex toys. Erotic games and fantasy intertwine here with a single objective: to foster the couple's intimate relationship.

And indeed, from what we learn from LoveLab's survey, 78% of couples who have used sex toys claim to have improved sexual harmony and satisfaction.

Lie down
The use of sex toys and cosmetics for the couple, also leads to the defusing of any sexual problems such as a reduction in desire or erection difficulties. In fact, not infrequently these types of disorders tend to become much more significant than they are. And this happens because one partner feels almost guilty or at fault towards the other, "guilty" of not being able to give (or feel) pleasure.

Instead, we forget that sex is intimacy and complicity and not a mechanical demand for orgasms. Playing together can represent the first step towards a healthier and, therefore, even more satisfying sexuality as a couple.

Forgetting, among other things, about "gender obligations": satisfying your partner means giving her a fully authentic sex life and not feeling under pressure because you are afraid of being insufficient. Thanks to sex toys you can experiment together and discover new ways of getting excited and satisfying your partner.

Choosing together increases complicity (and desire)
Even the choice of sex toys amplifies the intimacy of the couple and leads to emotional reconnection to the partner, in fact in the game and in the small transgressions you become accomplices again. From the vibrator to the lubricating gel, now the offer of erotic games is so wide that it can satisfy all tastes and all kinds of needs.

There's no need to suddenly throw yourself into a homemade "50 shades of grey": what counts is to satisfy your own desire and that of your partner, listening to each other and exploring each other spontaneously, without filters. Exploring the fantasies of the other, helps to get to know him better and maybe discover him differently.

And, why not, even more sexy and exciting. The novelty is a friend of sex life but novelty does not necessarily mean changing partners. Thanks to erotic games you can bring the news inside the couple, without compromising the union.

The History Of Sex Toys

The history of the vibrator is millennial. The first evidence appears in an archaeological record about 30,000 years ago. There are depictions of the use of sex toys in the findings of Ancient Egypt, Greece - *where in the fifth century BC they were called Olisbos and were for sale in the port of Miletus* - Rome, India and China (especially vaginal balls). The first real vibrator, however, was thanks to Cleopatra, not by chance passed into history as a great lover. Not enough for Caesar and Mark Antony, the story goes that in 54 B.C. she had devised a plan to give herself pleasure by herself: filling a closed pumpkin tube with mad bees that caused a slight vibration. Yes, because already at that time it was thought that the uterus was wandering around the body causing chaos, hence the word "*hysteria*", which comes from uterus.

You may not have known this, but the foundations for the creation of the first rudimentary vibrator models began in the 4th century BC. Hippocrates (a Greek doctor known as the father of Western medicine) claimed that a woman's uterus could become too light and dry due to lack of sexual intercourse. This condition was called "hysteria".

The great doctor Galen expanded the original definition of Hippocrates, stating that hysteria was caused by sexual deprivation especially in passionate women, virgins, nuns, widows and married women who had occasional sexual activity. The prevailing thought was that a woman's sexual frustration could be cured by an occasional session of massage of the female clitoris, helping to achieve orgasm.

Vibrators As a Therapy For Women's Well-Being

In the Middle Ages, the treatment of female sexual "hysteria" consisted in a sexual intercourse for married women, in marriage (obviously to have sex activities afterwards) for single women and widows in a vaginal massage by the midwife. At the dawn of the Victorian era, the diagnosis of "hysteria" was now common throughout Europe, symptoms could be traced back to weakness, nervousness, insomnia, water retention, abdominal heaviness, muscle spasms, shortness of breath, irritability, loss of appetite for food and sex and a "tendency to cause problems".

During the same period, doctors agreed that manual masturbation was difficult and tedious. Vibrators were born to meet medical sex hysteria therapies that involved achieving orgasm to overcome the problem.Since manual masturbation was too long and too expensive (obviously it had to be performed by the workers) the need for mechanical devices that could satisfy the sexual need arose. The vibrators drastically shortened the treatment time, increasing the doctors' business (obviously the economic gains) and eliminating the need to use midwives in this totally daring capacity.

The first vibrators had hydrotherapeutic mechanisms, where a hose with a high-pressure water jet was directed directly at the clitoris. For the vibrator, the step from the medical room to the bedroom was very short, especially with the advent of steam technology and especially electricity.

1900-1950:
In 1902, Hamilton Beach ® patented the first vibrator to take home, becoming one of the first home appliances, (just after the sewing machine and about ten years before the iron). These first models of vibrators were large, bulky and noisy. By 1917, there were more vibrators than toasters in American homes. During 1950, bedroom vibrators became a secret shared by the unexpressed masses of single women, housewives and couples.

1970-Today:
Thanks to the feminist movements of the 1970s, vibrators began to emerge from the shadow of embarrassment and shame. One of the most obvious signals of this change occurred in 1973, when Betty Dodson "invented" masturbation groups for women to "awaken their sexual consciousness". In the following years, vibrators were increasingly accepted by the culture: In 1990, surgeon general C. Everett Koop included vibrators as an option to practice safe sex.

The advent of online shopping has made it much easier and more discreet for people to buy vibrators, and women have had the opportunity to get to know vibrators through meetings at locals and organized at home. Today, vibrators have become a regular part of pop culture, often mentioned in books, magazines, TV shows, digital debates and daily conversations. In fact, 53% of American women and 45% of men have used a vibrator in their lives!

Sex Toys Types For Couples
How to reignite the dormant passion or give intimacy that extra pinch? If you've been asking yourself this question a lot lately, the time has come to dare and experiment with some tantalizing couple sex toys.

Generally considered instruments of pleasure for autoerotism, sex toys can actually prove to be very effective even in moments of intimacy with the partner, to rekindle the imagination and bring a little 'transgression under the sheets.

The only rule: both want to let go and experience something different.

And if only the classic vibrator comes to mind when you talk about sex toys, you'll have to think again: from the simple duvet to whet your appetite, to the handcuffs to experiment with soft bondage, to the vibrating rings to manage with the remote control, there are many erotic games to share in pairs. So here are the sex toys to try out with your partner for hot nights...

Vibrator

If you're vaginal, opt for vibrator. In the shape of a carrot, a cigar, or simply a penis, you'll be on the safe side. It's up to you to choose the shape that suits you. They can vary from 12 to 30 cm... be careful not to exaggerate!

As for the materials, you will be spoilt for choice: silicone, a hypoallergenic material that retains heat; jelly, very flexible and does not need to be disinfected; or cyberskin, loveclone or UR3, almost identical to human skin.

Hot little Animals

If you are a clitoral type, opt for the hot little animals: the best known is the vibrating duck. It will gently stimulate you and awaken your senses...

Teasing Feather

To tickle your imagination as well as the body, both yours and your partner's, a simple feather may be enough. Just touch it on your skin to discover new erogenous zones that you didn't even imagine you had. All to tickle.

Hot Dice

To rekindle your fantasy in bed, special dice such as those that can suggest the erotic positions to experiment as well as the actions to be performed on your erogenous zones can also be enough. The atmosphere will soon become incandescent.

The Hot Massager
Is an alternative to the classic vibrator, why not try the massager? The soft silicone one has different vibration modes and speeds to choose from. Very easy to use, you can have fun trying it in two. The Plus? The compact size that you can easily put in your suitcase and the practical bag in which to store it when you don't use it.

Soft Handcuffs
Bondage intrigues you, but would you rather start with something soft? Then it's off to the classic plush handcuffs with which you can have fun and unleash your hidden fantasies. Wrists or ankles... the choice is yours.

Geisha Balls
Also known as Kegel balls, they were born as gymnastics for the pelvic floor, becoming one of the most popular sex toys. Their use makes it easier to achieve orgasm, alone or in pairs, increasing pleasure.

Sex Toys: A Guide To Choosing The Right One
Sex toys are many and different in materials, sizes, and even prices: finding the right sex toy for you and your fantasies may not be easy, here are the useful advice.

Sex toy: where to buy it
In addition to the classic men's sex shops - where, however, many couples are also supplied and where you can also find objects with a more refined design - sex toys can also be found:

- in pharmacies, where the offer is quite limited...
- in the lingerie and underwear department of some department stores...
- in sex shops and online boutiques
- in erotic boutiques, where discretion and advice between women are guaranteed.

Choose the sex toy according to the area to be stimulated, how and with whom. The choice of a sex toy is extremely personal. So, before you buy a sex toy, you have to do a reconnaissance tour between your most intimate desires and your most hidden fantasies and ask yourself:

- Which area of your body do you want to stimulate: the clitoris? The G-spot? The B side? Or maybe several areas at once?

- How would you like to stimulate this area: there are not only vibrators!

- Who you want to use it with, where and in what situations: it is very important to define the style and size of the sex toy and to be able to take advantage of its services. For example, a rabbit vibrator might be great for solo use, but it might be too bulky if you're looking for something to put in your bag without too much embarrassment.

- Listen to your instinct: there must be some kind of lightning bolt between you and the sex toy that makes you say *"yes, you are the one!"*

Sex toy: choose by material

Always be informed about the materials of a sex toy, both for hygienic reasons and for the sensations that the different materials can give. Indeed:

- materials must be safe for health: the best are silicone, steel, borosilicate glass, pyrex, wood (especially ebony) and ceramics, which are easy to clean and sterilize and do not contain toxic substances.
- silicone is a fairly rigid material, but with heat it tends to soften and "adapts" to the body. At the same time, steel, ceramic, borosilicate glass and pyrex are very rigid materials, but give intense sensations and can be cooled or heated at will
- we do not recommend PVC, gelly or cyberskin sex toys, which may contain phthalates, substances harmful to the body that would be easily absorbed by the mucous membranes.

Sex toys: choose according to price

A sex toy must fit your taste and also your wallet. So ask yourself: *what kind of object do I want and how much do I want to spend?*

As far as style is concerned, we can count: the anatomical-realistic, decidedly explicit, the unsuspected, which hides the erotic function in disguise; the latest generation design, elegant and not too explicit, which reconciles functionality and aesthetics; the ironic, with funny shapes and bright colours; the luxury, with precious and expensive materials.

Prices range from a few dollars (for example, the disposable vibrating ring), to a few thousand in the case of gold or silver dildos and vibrators. Generally speaking, good quality products are affordable but not "for sales": it is often worth investing in a well-made object that you really like, rather than saving money and not being satisfied.

Sex toys: how they work

The modes and operation are not the same for all sex toys. Here is some useful information:

- Dildos don't vibrate, so they work "by hand" and are silent, vibrators may not.
- Vibrators can have one or more vibration intensities, a "fixed" vibration and/or different vibration paths that combine pulses of different intensities, some can be programmed and even go to music. Needless to say, more possibilities for enjoyment are better than one.
- Some vibrators also produce movements: those of the famous Twist&Shake are circular and particularly suitable to stimulate the G point.
- Vibrators can have different control modes: a wheel, buttons, a remote control with or - better - wireless.
- There are vibrators powered by batteries, rechargeable from the socket and rechargeable via USB port.
- Vibrators can: have a curvature to stimulate the G point (even dildos), be specific for the clitoris or the B side, be waterproof or wearable, stimulate multiple erogenous zones simultaneously.

Tips for use and storage

To fully enjoy the performance of a sex toy, it is advisable to use it with a lubricant (which you can buy with your toy):

- Water-based lubricants are suitable for use with condoms and all materials, but tend to dry out quickly;
- Silicone based lubricants provide more comfort, but are incompatible with condoms and silicone toys, which may deteriorate.
- Sex toys should be cleaned before and after each use, and should be stored carefully, both for hygienic reasons and to avoid damage and deterioration.

To do so, you can use a specific product (you can find them where you buy the toy), disinfectant and hypoallergenic. The silicone, steel, ceramic, glass and pyrex sex toys can also be sterilized with a more homemade but less practical method, i.e. in boiling water.

Sex toys: types to choose from

Finally, here is a short overview that will help you to orient yourself in the universe of sex toys to choose between fun, couple, superhitech etc., for all tastes

- Rabbit type double stimulation vibrator

- Multi-vibration pocket vibrator, suitable for both internal and clitoral stimulation
- Clitoris-specific vibrator
- Unsuspected vibrator: perhaps not the greatest pleasure, but it can also be used on the whole body. There are also "universal" vibrators, with a less fun look, which are suitable both for relaxing back or muscle massages and for intimate massages.
- Wearable clitoral vibrator, butterfly with panties, to stimulate the clitoris: another great classic. There are also pre-op versions for double stimulation or vaginal stimulation
- Dildo with suction cup base: can be attached to surfaces such as walls and floors
- G-spot specific dildo, thanks to its characteristic curvature
- Anal toys: they usually have rounded shapes and are made up of some spheres, they can be vibrating or not. Another example of anal toys is the butt-plug, with the characteristic wedge shape
- Sex toys for men: these are usually masseurs - vibrating or not - for prostate massage, penis rings (12) or "complements" to masturbation
- Sex toys for couples: They stimulate both partners and are suitable to experience some particular erotic situation.
- Geisha balls provide only a slight stimulation, but their virtue is to strengthen the pelvic floor, for longer, easier and more powerful orgasms.
- Whether they vibrate or not, cockrings or penis rings serve to improve and prolong erection and stimulate the clitoris during intercourse.

Below you will find our list of the best Sex Toys, surely you can find the one that suits you best!

17 + 1 Sex Toys For Intense Orgasms

No more classic vibrators: the new sex toys are eco-friendly, remote-controlled, rechargeable and innovatively designed! Here's an overview of the latest best in erotic games.

Ki-Wi

You don't eat it, but it could be forbidden fruit. It's not an animal, but it has an interesting long "nose". Ki-Wi is a stimulator for the Clit, which makes speed its most important feature, very silently tickling the most sensitive parts of the female body. It can also be used in water or the dark, because it is waterproof and glows in the dark... pure pleasure!

Nobessence

Some would say sex toys are something unnatural. To disprove skeptics and tempt lovers of ecology and renewable materials, the wooden dildos - indeed, the sculptures - produced by Nobessence are ideal. There are dildos in all shapes and for all tastes and if at some point you get tired of them and they don't warm you up anymore... they can be recycled in the fireplace. Although, personally, it would be a waste.

Zoon +

It is a wireless sex toy that can be used either at short distance with a remote control (for example: in a restaurant, supermarket...) or at thousands of kilometers controlling it from the website, even over oceanic distances.

Tor

The new jewel in LELO's collection is this vibrant ring, as precious as a solitaire but decidedly more suitable for couples' games, thanks to its two-hour charge (yes, it is rechargeable and not disposable) and its 6 (and I say 6) stimulation modes. After all, there are many ways to say "Yes".

Ina

Ina is not only a beautiful sex toy, it's a real bomb: a double action vibrator (internal and external) with 2 powerful vibrating motors for 8 different modes. What's new in this little toy with a refined Swedish design is the "circular mode" of the vibrations, which transfers a more intense stimulation first in one sensitive point, then in the other, creating a sensation of internal movement to reach explosive orgasms.

Squeel

It looks like the propeller of a motorboat, it's actually a sex toy that simulates oral sex thanks to its 10 silicone tabs that give a sea of orgasms. No need to add more.

Lovemoiselle

This brand new brand produces ceramic sex toys, a very, very interesting material: smooth as silk, it lends itself to pleasant games with temperature, from very cold to very hot. In the picture you can see two dildos, Noemie (pink) and Aveline (blue, which has a curvature to stimulate the G-spot), but there are also vibrators, always in ceramic.

Eve

An intimate masseur as light as a leaf, silky and elegant, which rests gently on the most sensitive points of the body, but manages to reverse the seasons: when the leaves fall, spring begins...of the senses.

Form 2

A small clitoral vibrator to hear a powerful stereo pleasure (each "ear" provides intense stimulation) with a compact and elegant sex toy. And water-resistant, for singing in the shower and bathtub. Rechargeable.

Better Than Chocolate

The name says it all: this clit vibrator is better than chocolate. Simple to use thanks to a user-friendly controller, it dispenses orgasms as if they were chocolates thanks to a very powerful and silent vibration, with different modes and speeds but, unlike chocolate, it doesn't melt in water: it resists up to a meter deep.

Pure Wand

This pure steel dildo has the curve in the right place to reach all the innermost secrets and make you touch the sky with a finger. And then it's beautiful, it's easy to clean (it's important, before and after each use!), the material is great to play with the temperature and experience very interesting sensations... it's no coincidence that it won an award for best "emerging" sex toy of 2009.

Bcurious

An ideal name for this small rechargeable vibrator with a very curious shape. It stimulates the clitoris by precisely tracing the contours of the female body to give an intense and silent pleasure. Suitable to act undisturbed in the bathtub (it is waterproof) or anywhere else, with 4 amazing stimulation modes. Not a comma is missing.

Contour Q
Okay. They're beautiful. But what are they for? They're a pair of porcelain "stones" to perform a modern version of the traditional stone massage. They are enclosed in the palm and slide over the whole body (even with the help of an oil) to release tension, caress sensitive areas and discover some unexpected points of pleasure thanks to the two stimulating surfaces, to be heated or cooled at will. Try it under the soles of your feet.

Teneo Uno and Duo
The smartballs of Fun Factory - a German company of excellence - are committed to improving the comfort and results of Kegel exercises that strengthen the pelvic floor muscles and improve orgasm. Hence the geisha balls Teneo 1, for beginners, and Teneo 2, for a more advanced level, both carved to give more pleasant sensations and get the most out of training.

Tickle-Popzzz
These lollipop-shaped vibrators could please Candy Candy, with their soft rubber suitable to pamper the most sensitive points of our body. A sweet pleasure without guilt and without arousing suspicion.

Kokeshi Dancer
These innocent dolls are actually waterproof massagers with 3 vibration speeds. Perfect to keep on the edge of the bathtub for fun water games, or undisturbed on the bedside table.

Sexy Bunny
Follow the pink rabbit and the orgasms will be a wonder. This vibrator - in slang "dual action vibe" or "rabbit", just like the one that caused a certain... addiction to Charlotte in Sex & the City - combines clitoral and vaginal stimulation with a fun pink & punk design.

Cry baby
The tears, of course, are dictated by emotion. Here is the prince of vibrating eggs: ten programs and no strings. Just use the remote control to tune into

the right frequency... Special for playing in pairs, especially outside the bedroom. Now it's up to you to let your imagination run wild.

Sex Toys: 5 Taboos To Break

Sex toys are not just vibrators, they are not used exclusively during autoerotism, they are not addictive, they do not replace anything or anyone and they are not "dirty" games. This is how the false myths about sex toys collapse, with the expert opinion.

Only a fool would think that sex toys are no longer taboo for the simple reason that for some time now they have been sold in pharmacies, with the much more aseptic name of personal masseurs, and in department stores or luxury boutiques as objects of pleasure. The prejudices, the false myths, last so long that they seem to be lovers of tantra, skillfully hovering between underground legend and skepticism.

There are those who think that once you feel the sensations given by a vibrator then you can't do without them and that normal sex becomes bland, there are those who see sex toys as a placebo to calm the hot spirits of perverse minds and unsatisfied singles and there are men who feel threatened by a silicone dildo that would like to banish it from the bed and fantasies of the girlfriend, and so on. Nothing could be more wrong!

Personally I find them to be very amusing objects, often useful, certainly pleasant. The quality of the experience also depends on how and with whom you use them. Not that you need to be MacGayver to make them work, but it's the spirit that counts: something much more complex than any mechanical gadget.

1 - Sex toys are not only vibrators
Of course, they are the most common in the collective imagination and sometimes this word is used to indicate toys in general, but those who believe that only vibrators exist will be amazed by a world of dildos, clitoral stimulators, vibrating rings and curious, sometimes unsuspected shapes...

2 - Sex toys are not only for single use

Using them alone is fun and helps you get to know yourself, discover and fantasize, try new sensations and relax. But playing with two people is twice as much fun as the erogenous zones and, above all, many more ideas: a practically endless combination of fantasies and pleasure.

3 - Sex toys are not addictive

Vibrations are not addictive and do not make flesh sex insensitive, on the contrary. Sex toys are potential sensory amplifiers that do not give normal sex "tolerance" at all. Learning more about your body and its reactions creates much more detailed mental maps of arousal and therefore improves your sensitivity. Some female "vacuum devices", devices that create a slight vacuum and help to draw blood into the mucous membranes of the small lips have been indicated by the FDA (the very strict US pharmaceutical medical control body) for female arousal disorders.

4 - Sex toys are not a substitute of the male or "natural" sex

Using sex toys does not mean being dissatisfied with your man, your friend or your sex life, and they are a great way to interact with your partner. The very fact of going to buy them together or making a surprise opens up scenarios that move away from routine, which is the real risk of unsatisfactory sexuality. If, on the other hand, he feels replaced and belittled by toys, reassure him: sex toys and human anatomy are different things, therefore not comparable. If at all possible, they can be integrated, experiencing new pleasures because "imagination has no boundaries".

5 - Sex toys are not dirty games

In fact, they must always be cleaned, washed before and after each use. Forget the word games, it is absolutely not said that sex toys are something sleazy, pornographic, to be used without feeling, without love. Instead, they can be engaging instruments of love and participation in moments of romance. In short, even vibrators have a heart, if the person who uses them has one.

P.S. *Everyone is - indeed: must be - free to choose how to live their sexuality and eros according to their tastes and beliefs, so to use sex toys as to ignore them. But I firmly believe that with the mind clear of false myths, much more cumbersome than an erotic toy, you choose much better.*

ANAL SEX
Anal Sex: Normal or Not?
Is having anal sex normal? Do you have a good time? Why haven't I tried it before? These are the standard questions that many ladies ponder.

In actuality, the pleasure you receive from anal intercourse is determined by your willingness to attempt.

There's nothing stopping you from attempting anything as long as you're comfortable with it.

It's your body, your decision, your life; you're the only one who knows what's best for your body and sexuality.

An Introduction to Anal Sex

Before we talk of some of the best positions and how to make the most anal sex, it is vital to know some precautions and set ground rules. It is crucial because, unlike the regular vagina sex, you need to exercise the right kind of caution.

Take the anal training before going the whole way.

We do not recommend starting anal sex unprepared. Remember, if you have never had anything in your anus, straight away, asking for a penis to make way might not be the smartest of moves. The right thing to do is to experiment a little with small sex toys. This is important as it will stimulate and trigger the anal muscles, and your body will be much better prepared to take in the penis. Do not create a fuss, and be ready for a little anal training that can help you stay put for the big round of anal sex.

Have an in-depth mutual discussion

They will not perform anal sex if only one of the partners is willing. Remember, this is the type of sex in which both parents must be on the same page. If any of the partners experience extra pain or discomfort during the time between anal sex, you should immediately stop having sex. Don't make each other's lives difficult. The goal is to enjoy sex, have fun, and not appear to be a punishment.

The lube is mandatory

Always remember that there is a lot of difference between the vagina and the anus. The vagina has been so designed that it tends to self-lubricate when aroused. However, the anus doesn't work like that. So, if you do not want to bleed profusely and feel discomfort, the intelligent thing to do is to ensure that you use plenty of water-based lubes. Doing this can make the whole process smooth and better. No matter how messy and dirty it gets, slather as much lube as needed and then go for the significant penetration.

Steers clear of numbing creams

There are plenty of people who tend to choose numbing creams for the simple reason that they can take away the pain which is associated with anal sex.

However, you genuinely need to understand that those creams can be potentially harmful in the long run.

When you use such numbing cream, your anus would be completely numb, so even if the penetration is too deep or there is an injury, you won't be able to feel and tell. This, in turn, could be the cause of several other problems. Until and unless you are willing to tolerate the pain, do not go for anal sex.

Try non-penetrative version first

When doing anal sex for the first time, you do not necessarily need to push the whole penis through. Remember, sex is more about the experience than the complete act of doing it. So, if you want to prepare your body and enjoy anal sex repeatedly, we want you to start slow. You could do things like fingering or oral sex but do not get ahead with penetration.

This way, you prepare your body and your mind for what is likely to follow. After a few rounds of oral teasing, maybe you could try penetrative sex in the next session. This will also prepare your anal muscles in a much better inner.

Never leave home without a condom.

You must understand that there is no way you can function without a condom. When it comes to anal sex, however, the chances of transmitting STDs and other infections are extremely high. Make sure the man is always wearing a condom.

Foreplay is important

When it comes to anal sex, do not get started with penetration immediately. Like we have been emphasizing already, you have to engage in a fair deal of foreplay to prepare your body and anal muscles for the big event which will follow. There is plenty of foreplay and oral sex options that you could fiddle with and warm up for the big session.

Maintain the basic hygiene

When we are dealing with anal sex, make sure to maintain the basic level of hygiene. So, if you are using sex toys, you will keep them clean. Similarly, trim your nails and wash your hands before and after anal sex. Often, these little steps ensure that you won't contaminate your body, and you can prevent the transmission of borne bacterial diseases as well.

Once you are mindful of these factors, it will be relatively much more accessible and significantly safer to proceed with anal sex.

Anal activities

There are different activities that you could, alone or with your partner.

Anal sex

Well, this is self-explanatory. I suggest starting with doggy style or with the receiver lying on the back. These are the most accessible position and allow for the maximum spread of the area.

Prostate stimulation

Guess what, men G-Spot is the prostate, and it can be reached through anal stimulation. There are specific toys designed to stimulate the prostate on the market, but it can be done with your fingers as well. The important thing is to use a good amount of lube and take it at your own pace. Finding the prostate is not complex; you could do this massage yourself or with the help of your partner.:

· Apply lube.

· Insert the index finger slowly to the first knuckle, to it a couple of times applying lube.

· When you feel the area is well-lubricated, insert up to the second knuckle and repeat the previous steps until you reach the third knuckle.

· Once the finger is comfortably inserted, search for a rounded lump roughly 4 inches inside the rectum and up towards the root of the penis. This is the prostate, and it is extremely sensitive.

· You can massage the prostate in a circular motion or back and forth but gently.

Pegging

This practice is fantastic and gives the woman an incredible sense of power. It consists of penetrating her man with a strap-on dildo. For pegging, a double ending dildo can be used; one side can penetrate the anus while the other is inserted in the vagina. I have tried this practice with my man a few times, and we both loved it. Start with a double-ended dildo. There are strap-ons on the market that do not require any harnesses, but I have personally found hard to use them. I do prefer the harness version, which is much more stable. Also, consider buying one with a vibration function for extra pleasure.

Butt plugs

They can be an excellent addition to your sex life; butt plugs are specifically designed to be inserted into the rectum, even for long periods. These toys are generally smooth and short and can be used during sex by both men and women to provide additional stimulation to the rectum. So if you want to try some light butt stuff and have a different stimulation during sex, butt plugs are what you are looking for.

The Anal Sex Positions to Try

The following description of each position is not intended to be the definitive "correct way to go." when trying something completely new, it is best to experiment in familiar and straightforward positions not to complicate the process. The correct part is crucial for anal beginners; It will help you get used to this exciting new form of stimulation and pleasure. Each of the following positions has its advantages and disadvantages, and each is suitable for newbies and newbies. Remember that most places are ideal for couples: any gender or sexual orientation. Remember, there is no wrong sexual position if it works for you and your partner. Feel free to adjust the settings described in this part to suit your specific needs, including your height, flexibility, comfort, and personal preferences.

Sitting Dog

Lean forward from the lap dance position until your upper body is at right angles to his. Try facing a wall or another (sturdy!) Bench in front of you so that you have something to lean on or hold on to. That provides you with a more extraordinary view of your buttocks and a better angle of penetration, especially if your penis curves away from your body. That is good for a less extreme version of the doggie style.

Flying Doggie

In Flying Doggie, she kneels on all fours on the bed, and he stands (instead of kneeling) behind her. She brings her legs together, and his legs are on either side as he penetrates her from a little higher.

Doggy Angle

When you lift your bum in the air and lower your head or head and shoulders, your body tilts perfectly to stimulate your G-spot, which can be more comfortable for some women than standing on all fours.

Froggie

Froggie Position is a variation on cowgirl in which she crouches on her feet. That gives her more freedom to ride it vigorously and puts less strain on her knees, but she works for multiple muscle groups, so she has to be fit to keep it up. She can put her hands on her stomach in preparation. That position can be easier to achieve on the floor than in bed, depending on the firmness of the mattress and possible leverage.

Reverse Froggie

Start in Reverse Cowgirl, stand up to crouch, sit straight, or lean forward, do most pushing work to get into this position. The woman must be fit, flexible, and have strong quadriceps to hold this position. Leaning forward, you can caress your partner's eggs and soft perineum; If he likes anal play, she can reach into his anus for stimulation and penetration. It can also be tilted backward for better skin contact and a different angle of penetration.

Standing

When standing, both partners stand in the same direction, and he steps into her from behind. It can stand upright, leaning against a wall, or leaning against a piece of furniture.

Upright Missionary

She lies on her back in the upright missionary position; he sits on her knees and stands between her legs. She bends her knees and rests her feet on his chest; in this position, he can stroke and squeeze her breasts or even pinch her nipples when he likes it; You can also easily reach and stimulate her clitoris with your hand or a vibrator. You will have a great view of the action in this position as you can see your penis going in and out. She can watch him penetrate her. and caress her breast and nipples. This can be an alternative to Missionary when taking the weight off her or in a less pretzel-like body position; it's also suitable for members of very different sizes or weights.

Missionary L

He sits on his knees and moves between her legs; she lies on her back and puts her legs up in front of him so that they are perpendicular to the rest of her body and form an L at right angles to the torso and the rectum slightly straightens up and makes penetration a little easier. In Missionary, where your legs are bent back, you need to be pretty flexible to hold this position, so this may not be a position for many women. It can last a long time. This position allows him a shallower penetration than other variations, which is good if he has a longer penis or if he doesn't like it too deep.

Spoon and Fork

To test this variation, pairs should start in the spoon position. Next, she puts her left leg under his right leg and her right leg over it to wrap it around his waist. He can lower his arm to give himself. more leverage and more thrust. Like the spoon, this position creates shallower penetration and is ideal for men with long penises; However, many men find that they can push faster and with more enthusiasm. Since her body leans more towards him, kissing is more accessible in this position too.

The Jockey Sex

Those women enjoy having their men in their corner and making the most of this type of sex. The woman must lie down in this position with her legs tight. The man would then come up behind you and sit with his knees bent.

He needs to lean over the back to get the best angle for pushing his penis inside your butthole and driving you insane with his rocking to and from movement.

So, these are some of the best anal sex positions which you can surely try. Remember, it is essential to observe the proper rules, which we had discussed earlier. Practicing safe sex is crucial to ensure that both partners can benefit from it.

This is not the ultimate bible, as there are endless other positions that you can try. So come up with anything out of your mind. The only rule is that never stop having fun!

If you are up for a round of anal sex, you could try some of these positions and note down your experience. You will prepare better for the best sex experience of all time.

Highchair

This is one of the powerful anal sex positions which is likely to give you both a lot of thrill. The woman needs to sit on a chair so that the butt must stick out of it. The guy then needs to stand behind. He could kneel down or even squat based on the elevation of the chair.

The man would grab his partner's waist and slowly push his penis in the anus. The in and out moment is sure to feel like a rocking chair and will drive both of you crazy with passion.

Reverse Isis

In the reverse Isis position, he lies with his legs apart and slightly bent; she sits between his legs, with her face at his feet, leaning forward on his knees with her legs together. Until her breasts touch his legs, he can sit up to move into the doggy position.

The Split

In The Split, she puts herself in the lap dance position, but instead of putting her legs between his, she puts them on either side of his, with your toes, which limits your ability to ride it hard. Keeping your legs together will further restrict your movements.

The Burning Man

Yet another position wherein the man achieves the dominant role, and you could play the submissive lead.

The position is simple, but you would need a tabletop or even a sofa. The woman needs to lean on the top of the couch, table, or bed so that her anal end out. The man then spoons you from behind, and after enjoying some oral sex, he pushes his cock inside your hole. Therefore, it is essential to ensure that your table or sofa is such that it doesn't hurt you when leaning on it. Keeping a pillow or a blanket might be a good alternative.

This form of anal sex has the potential to get rough as your man could do all he wishes since you are bent on the table and can only moan and shriek in pleasure and pain. So, for those who love rough sex, this is

YabYum

YabYum is a classic tantric sex position in which one partner sits on the other's lap and faces each other; However, it is generally taught and practiced as a position for vaginal penetration; it also works very well for anal penetration. The man is sitting with his legs slightly crossed, and the woman is sitting on his lap, encircling her legs around his waist and torso. You can use firm pillows under your thighs if you need more support for your legs. With his legs crossed, he can stand her in front of him. If you need back help, you can lean against the wall or the headboard. When she is lying on your lap, she can rise slightly above her knees, and you should bend her forward, pelvis forward to make your anus more accessible. He can hold the base of his penis to help her, and she can slowly lower herself onto him. That is a relaxing and meditative position. So once you are in it, you shouldn't feel any tension or tension. As you do this, adjust yourself to sink into place comfortably.

The Chairman

Try entering YabYum on a chair, ottoman, sofa, or pillow on the floor. A comfortable chair or sofa can give men the back support they need. With a firmer surface under him and legs down, a man can feel firmer in this position, with more freedom of movement and a little more ability to squeeze gently. A man can hold his partner's hips and move his body up and down on his penis. If the partner is seated in a sufficiently broad chair, she can move her legs so that she straddles him but is not wrapped around his waist.

Lap Dance

The edge of the bed, but it is best if both partners' feet can lightly touch the floor. The man is sitting on a chair, sofa, or ottoman, and his partner is astride him (with her back to him). He holds her legs apart, and she sits between his legs with her legs together. The closer she is to the ground, the easier she can achieve complete freedom of movement. That is a good position for couples where the woman is much smaller than the man.

Tailgate

In surfing language, tailgate means paddling out into the ocean with your surfboard to catch a wave or follow someone else. She lies on her stomach in the tailgate position with her legs slightly apart. She, with his legs on either side of hers, penetrates her from behind. If he's having trouble getting in, she can tilt her hips toward him for the first penetration and then lie down. Once inside of her, he pushes his legs together. He sets the tone in this position and takes care of the depth and rhythm of the penetration. You can also start in the Doggie Style, Doggie Angle, or Spooning position and quickly switch to them.

Horizontal Tailgate

It starts in the seated tailgate position, and once stepped onto it, lean forward to lie on it with your legs outstretched (A). That allows for more skin-to-skin contact, and many women like to feel their partner's weight on them. It can also increase your partner's feeling of being "taken over." He can kiss her neck and ears and whisper sweet or naughty things to her (B). There are some downsides: a horizontal tailgate may not be feasible if he is taller and can't support his weight. Some women may also feel too cramped or uncomfortably immobilized regardless of their size. It has even less pressure.

The Turtle Position

This position is for those couples who like to play the submissive-dominant game. The woman needs to be on her knees and then pull them inside. This position gives her hips a high arch, and the man could kneel and draw her waist towards him before pushing his penis in the anus and giving her a fun-filled ride.

This position can be uncomfortable for the woman, and you should be ready to improvise the moment you want to.

Stallion

In stallion, she stands with her legs apart, then bends forward at the waist and leans on the bed (or other furniture), and he stands behind her. Stallion has all of the benefits of the doggie style with more strength as he has total leverage with his hips and legs. For some couples, this may work better than Flying Doggie due to its size and height. If she is feeling too much tension on her knees in other doggie positions, this is a better option for her. he can position his hips a little higher than hers and indirectly stimulate her G-spot when he penetrates her.

The Pearly Gates

If you are looking for an anal sex position that could feel a little exciting, this is it. In this position, the man needs to lie down on his bed. He can spread apart his legs a little, but the feet should be pretty planted. The woman would now get on top of the man and face the same side. Make sure to position yourself in such a way that the man's penis could find the woman's butthole, and he could slowly but steadily make an entry and please you thoroughly.

This position allows for a lot of cuddling, foreplay, and even fingering as well. So, feel free to elevate your senses before getting downright dirty and rough.

Side Saddle

She lies on her side with straight knees, legs together, and at an angle to the body. On his knees, he steps into her from the side. Think of Side Saddle as a combination of doggie style and spooning. Because of its unique position, you have the most control over-penetration.

The Y

Starting in the side saddle, she moves her upper leg up to rest on her shoulder, essentially creating a side split with her body. Unlike the side-saddle, the Y requires strength and flexibility from her side, and some women can be difficult; or This variant allows both partners better access to your vulva and a good view of the penetration.

Stairway to Heaven

Stairway to Heaven is the standing position performed on the stairs. Ladders provide handrails (and possibly a nearby wall) for support and balance, adding stability and leverage to both partners—the right height.
undoubtedly an excellent position to try.

Over the Edge

Imagine Over the Edge as a horizontal tailgate on the edge of the bed. She lies on her stomach, her head, shoulders, and upper body hang over the edge of the bed, her hands are on him, he is lying on top of her, her hands also flat on the floor. Both partners in this position may have a head frenzy (of blood and oxygen), which in some may exacerbate sexual sensations. Your breasts won't tighten in this position, and you may feel less claustrophobic. That works best when your bed is relatively low off the floor.

Best Kamasutra Positions for Anal Sex

The Pivot Position

The girl, during intercourse, turns like a horizontal wheel around a vertical axis right around the male. The male caresses her and pinches her breasts, benefiting from those positions. For her part, the reclining man, whose penis uses her as a pivot in blood and flesh, can fondle her chest. She just takes up the length of his penis by squirming and raising herself a bit; she needs to believe in herself. The position of the pivot" will allow women and men to enjoy a great mental focus. For males who have begun to practice sexual continence, that is the reason why this position is proposed.

Seesawing Position

Sitting slightly in front of the thighs of the male, she only takes part of his penis so that the length inserted alternately can be easily managed by either of them. She can stroke the male's legs kneeling; he comes to reach her halfway or perhaps behaves as though he was going to withdraw entirely by supporting himself on his arms and making quick thrusts with his pelvis, living her almost fully to be able to enter her open vagina again, and that is very wet in this position. This gives her an incredibly good upward massage.

The Buttering Position

The man, firmly planted in the rear opening, turns around as if he is in a position to support his body on the palms as well as on the tip of the toes. In this position, in addition to circular ones, the male can make come-and-go movements. The female will not remain passive but will respond with smooth pelvic movements based on those created by the male.

The male provides the female with an exceptional massage of her G spot in the "buttering" position so that not many females can resist such stimulation without getting a deep orgasm (we're talking about non-ejaculatory orgasm, of course) as such. If the male thinks that he is approaching the orgasm, he must stop moving and concentrate his attention on the central position 3to be able to sublimate the sexual energy. This is also available to the woman.

The Hidden Door Position

The male lies on the female. She encompasses his thighs, ready to take him as much as the hilt. He insinuates himself deeply and softly anchored within her, where he cuddles her, stroking her back, hips, and breasts. She draws up her spreads and legs them somewhat to have the freedom to give her vulva to the g absolutely to the needs of her lover even more.

Nevertheless, in an analogous situation, if he knows she loves anal penetrations, the male lover can even entertain himself with his lover's anal opening in case he knows she loves anal penetrations. Here the female can relax in the very best way as well as the male has full control over the penetration of his penis into the hot and constricted opening, which she gives him with confidence and affection.

This position is the right to lift the sexual energy and sublimate it in pure love. To achieve this elevated emotion—love that is pure, the lovers have not to focus on genital gratification during this position, but they have to concentrate their attention on the heart area and be aware of the flying feeling that this position actually creates if the lovers later let themselves to concentrate on the heart area.

The Caress of the Bud Position

Lying on the stomach and the legs interlaced, the male and the female turn to each other with their backs. However, for a few males whose thick and short penis can only be flexed with difficulty, the particular effect of this position can be quite painful. The female, who retains her balance with a single-arm now facing her lover and who is assisted in the continuation of the position, the female, who maintains her balance with a single-arm now facing her lover and who's supported on the male's body, is titillated at the entrance to her vagina by the glans. Obviously, this is only foreplay to deeper coitus. The male can inserts his erect penis into the vagina by turning gently to one side. The vagina is now ready to get it in its totality.

For those lovers who are beginners in the art of sexual energy management, this position is the right one. The position of "the caress of the bud" allows lovers the ability to be much more mindful of the strength of pleasure and to reduce it by stopping the movement when they think they are near the climax. The sexual energy they have to concentrate their attention on is in the middle of the forehead for sublimation. This will trigger a clear-minded state in both lovers, which will allow them to regulate sexual power as well as to sublimate far higher energies.

The Seesaw Position

Lovers are facing one another. The male then brings the female to the level of his waist. She's always able to catch him by his arms or around his neck, maybe. Penetrated by the entire length of the penis, she allows the erect shaft to slip through her narrow vagina. By squeezing her legs tightly around his waist, the male can press and embrace her very close to himself that she can simplify for him.

In this particular position, with the aid of the strength of her muscles, the penis massages the entire vagina, the female can make good going and coming movements in tune with those of her lover. Both women and men would experience immense joy in this way. To be able to stay away from the male's ejaculatory orgasm as well as the female's discharge orgasm, both lovers have to really direct the sexual energy along the spine towards the crown. In pure love and happiness, this will create a sublimation of simple energy.

The Closed and Opened Ring Position

Here we have two complete submission positions, where the female gets the male and then the degree of its resemblance. According to his rhythm, he penetrates her effortlessly, entertaining himself by inserting and removing his penis, sometimes carefully and sometimes violently. An experienced woman in the art of lovemaking is going to use this position to swing gently and carefully with her own thighs on the thighs of her lover and to send her vagina, which is really being bombarded from below.

The closed and opened ring sex position helps the male to be even more conscious of the strength of pleasure and to reduce it by stopping the movements when he knows he's approaching the climax. Both lovers have to concentrate their attention in the center of the forehead for sublimation, their sexual energy. This will trigger a clear-minded state in both lovers, which will allow them to concentrate their focus to sublimate.

The Ripe Mango Plum Position

The male plunges into her with great sensitivity to begin spinning motions with his penis even more aggressively, and that is pretty fascinating for both lovers. He sits over his lover to penetrate deeper, spreads his legs, and inserts his penis into the swollen mango plum, which is well supplied by the adroit massage with blood. For both lovers, this sexual pose is an extremely arousing one. The elevated pelvis position of the female allows the sexual energy to "rush" into the region of the thyroid gland. This can cause an exceptionally high form of orgasm in females.

To stay away from his ejaculatory orgasm or maybe her discharge of orgasm, the male needs to stop his movements as he thinks he or maybe she's getting close to the climax. This sex position helps the ripe mango plum to sublimate sexual energy into ingenuity and purity.

The Door Ajar Position

The male will keep his lover by the hips, after which he gently pushes it back between the legs of his lover. The female, pivoting slightly to the side, reaches around the neck of her lover in order not to lose any of the lengths of the penis. Well lubricated from other positions, the vulva is now moistened, allowing the penis to slip easily, massaging the vagina's sides. To be able to keep away from the ejaculatory orgasm of the male as well as the extreme orgasm of the female, both lovers have to concentrate their attention in the forehead. They will become much more aware of the sexual energy in this particular way.

The Face to Face Position

Leaning on her soles and palms, the woman raises her pelvis so that the male can insert his penis into her vagina. He can capture his lover's waist with a single or even despite both hands while he has kneeled. This position helps lovers to search for each other to explore how their lust mounts and express their affection. The woman can gently push her pelvis, tuning her movement with the going and coming motions of the male. She can stretch her legs primarily to be able to take up the entire length of the penis of her partner.

If the male thinks he's getting close to the ejaculatory climax, he's going to stop moving and concentrate his focus in the central position to be able to sublimate the sexual energy. This is also available to the woman.

The Top Position

This will make her lie on her back, sustained and blocked by the thighs of the male who penetrates her in a controlled press up, tightly massaged on the sides of the female, taking up the entire length of the penis. At the moment, he allows his weight to fall on her a lot more as he wants to feel a lot more satisfaction. The woman can feel him more deeply at exactly the same time. This position gives both lovers intense gratification and amplifies the sexual force. This is why it does not start contact with beginners in the art of lovemaking with sexual continence. Both lovers must concentrate their attention on the central position.

When the woman thinks that her lover gets close to the climax, she must avoid the movements of the male and simply press firmly on the middle of the forehead with her thumb. Therefore, his attention will be taken to the forehead region from the genital area, which helps to increase the sexual tension along the backbone.

Conclusion

If you're up for a round of anal sex, you may try any of these options and, as always, keep track of your experience. It will better prepare you for the best sex experience of your life.

DIRTY TALK

Introduction

During sex, dirty talk can really help in arounding the mood during intercourse. Expert therapists have discovered that filthy talk during sex may really improve love making. Many couples now use this as a technique for not only obtaining sexual pleasure and quick climax, but things may also get hotter and more fascinating in a bedroom.

What is Dirty Talk?

Even though it may sound like a silly question to ask, for some women, they still need a little bit more information on what dirty talking is all about before they even dare to try it out. This is just part of human nature; before we are willing to try something, we want to make sure that we are good at it first. This is exactly how you feel. Before you even dare to WOW your man with some dirty talk in bed to send him over the edge. The last thing that you want to do is totally kibosh a hot moment and end up looking like a total doofus. That just isn't going to happen to you.

So, what is dirty talk? Well, it is just as it sounds. It is bedroom language that we use to communicate our wants, desires and needs to each other. Sometimes, it is even used to communicate a thought or used as a compliment. There really isn't just one particular way to define dirty talk because it is different for all couples.

Even though it sounds daunting at the moment, when you learn how to dirty talk and how to feel more comfortable with it, you and your man will both develop your own form of bedroom talk that will send you both over the edge.

Now, this is the biggest problem that women find themselves in when it comes to dirty talk - they can't get over the nervousness. Yes, it is nerve wracking to become vocal for the first time in the bedroom when you normally aren't used to it, but this is where we all thrive. When we are taken outside of our comfort zones, this is when we all really start living and really start enjoying sex for what it is worth.

You can't expect your sex life to flourish if you are constantly staying within your boundaries. Learning to experiment a bit outside of those boundaries, is really exciting and will lead to more pleasurable sessions in the bedroom.

So, how do you get over the nervousness? Well, it won't happen overnight. The best way to start to get more comfortable with dirty talk is to start off with sexting.

Sexting involves using your phone to send dirty text messages to your man. They can be anywhere from PG rated all the way to adult rated words. I would recommend to always start off light. Then, you can start to make things get hotter as you get more comfortable. Start off by telling him how much you can't wait to see him later or how sexy you think he is. That will help you to get more cozy with the idea of upping the language and using some raunchier vocabulary.

Once sexting feels like a breeze, then it is a good idea to start talking more during sex. The best way to start off is to compliment your man or to tell him what feels good as it is happening. Then, you will get used to using your voice during sex and this will make future bouts of dirty talk come a lot more naturally and effortlessly to you, resulting in fabulous bedroom talk that gets both you and your man more and more aroused.

Don't fret if the nervousness continues to last. You are doing something that is not the norm for you so it is only natural that you are going to feel uneasy. Don't worry though, practice makes perfect and the more you do it, the easier it will be!

So, now that you are ready and feeling a bit more confident with some sexting examples and light dirty talk in bed, what is next?

Well, naturally, you are working towards a goal of creating a distinct love language between you and your man. In order to do this, you need to start dirty talking in the first place, because, let's face it - this is up to you to get going.

Dirty talk is a lot sexier when women do it and yes, it will be hot when your man starts doing it, but he probably won't engage in it until you take the lead, so it is up to you to start it.

The Implications of Dirty Talking

Talking dirty does not imply that you force yourself to do so. Here is not the place to think creatively. It only suggests that you be yourself during sex. Every human being has a filthy side within him or her. It solely depends on how easygoing you are. You must be yourself and speak your mind. You have nothing to hide, so don't stutter between your words. A fresh mind can not only entice your lady, but it can also lighten your heart.

The Effects of Dirty Talking

This strategy may also be used to kick-start love-making before ex. Without really or overtly requesting for sex, highly dirty language or sexy talk might entice your spouse. It can effectvely activate your exual deire or exual part of your body before you are touched. It acts as a sex appetitizer, similar to taking a cup of coffee before a formal dinner. Exy talk can demolih fear in one's thoughts and allow them to get one teep higher from a mental standpoint. It can also help you stop your hyne and hesitation, have an open mind, and be honest with yourself.

How to Talk Dirty

Dirty language during sex may be used to flatter your wife. As previously said, this would undoubtedly turn on a lady physically. Try to appreciate her private bits as much as possible. Make her realize that if she cooperates and enjoys, you may be more and more naughty.

You'll notice that most girls like naught boys and nasty talk if you practice these techniques. It goes without saying that having filthy conversations during sex might have a negative impact on your love life.

The Right Way

A lot of women wish they knew how to talk dirty the right way. It would make things so easy on them in bed if they only knew what their man wanted them to say and how he wanted them to say it. You can start talking dirty to your man the right way, in a way that will drive him wild, with just a little know-how. It's not as hard as you think to do this right, and let's face it, most men love to hear their ladies talk like porn stars in bed. You can do this just as well as any of those porn stars can do, because it's merely talking. It's a skill anyone can learn. Take your sex life into the stratosphere by learning about dirty talk today.

The fact is, timing and tone matter almost as much as what you say. You have to get it all just right, and if you don't have a natural sense for these things, it can feel awkward to try to talk dirty. Have you ever whispered something you thought was dirty into your man's ear during sex only to have him laugh heartily? This happens, and it's not your fault. It's just that you haven't been taught how to talk dirty properly.

First and foremost, any dirty talk you do needs to be completely natural. Don't try to force it, because it will sound fake and that is a big turn-off to a guy. He wants it to be real. Men get very caught up in the idea of their sexual prowess turning on their woman, and it turns them on to think that they're doing it. If you sound fake when dirty talking to him, he'll feel inadequate in bed and this will be upsetting to him. So, only say dirty things if you're REALLY feeling them.

One of the best things you can do is ask him questions. If you feel moved to do something sexy for him, ask him in your most sexy, alluring voice (while looking directly into his eyes) if that is what he wants you to do. For example, if you want to give him oral sex, tell him what you want to do and then ask him if that's what he wants you to do? Go over a few of the juicier details, getting his answer after each 'point'. Don't drag it out into a long list of 35 different questions, 3 or 4 is more than enough for you to use a few choice dirty words as well as keying up his anticipation of what's to come. Say it just right, and really mean it, and your man will practically do backflips to please you in return.

Next, touch him when you talk dirty. The personal contact will make the dirty talk even more alluring. Finally, try to include really filthy words, because guys love this. Instead of using the normal, clinical and boring words for the various sexy parts of your bodies, use the ones that sound and feel most erotic, daring and dirty to you. It's the best gift you can give your guy in bed. If you know how to talk dirty the right way, there's nothing he won't do for you in return.

How To Turn Her On

In order to please a woman and make her want you more, getting her turned on is the single most important aspect of every sexual encounter. Luckily, there are many ways to go about achieving this. Following are just a few of those various techniques that can ensure your woman gets in the mood as often as you wish.

(1) Make her feel good

A woman's main sexual organ is her brain. The best and most effective way to turn her on is to make her feel good, relaxed and sexy. No matter how busy you can be, this step is not to be skipped. Going straight for the lower part of her body when her brain or mind is not yet ready can only turn her off.

For many women, getting in the mood requires being both emotionally and physically ready. Do not rush. Instead, you take the time to stroke her hair, rub her shoulders and basically just hold and touch her. When you are out in public, you hold her hand. Make sure you tell her that you find her to be beautiful and sexy.

Also do take the time to kiss her neck. Just press the tip of your tongue against her skin and kiss her softly. Kissing any part of the neck will get a woman in the mood. Do not miss her ear lobes, the back of her ears. Lightly nibble and kiss on these areas can also arouse her a lot.

(2) Seduce her with dirty talking

This is another good way to seduce her brain and make a woman turned on. Do not be creepy about it and try not to be too vulgar unless you know that it gets her in the mood. Lean in close and whisper into her ear all of the things that you have thought about doing to her. For example, if you and your partner both enjoy it when you perform oral sex on her, try describing it from your point of view. Talk about how much you love touching her body and how it feels like to touch her with your tongue. The more descriptive you can get, the better dirty talk will be.

Once your partner is aroused, you can start complimenting her body. For the best dirty talk, do not say general things. Instead, you focus on one particular area of her body and describe it in detail, including what you like about it. For example, you can sit between her legs and talk about how you like to watch her open and close them.

Another dirty talk technique you can use is simply telling your partner all those naughty sexual thoughts you have, such as watching her perform oral sex on another woman. Because this is pure fantasy, you know this is something that is unlikely to happen in real life and neither do you want it to happen. Encourage your partner to share her sexual fantasies. The more open you are, the easier it will be for her to let loose. Lightly kiss her on the ear from time to time while telling her all these. Do not spoil the mood by sticking your tongue in her ear in a rough way.

(3) Tease her with aphrodisiacs

Confucius once said over 5,000 years ago, "Food and sex are part of human nature." Therefore when it comes to making a woman horny, one of the most effective ways is to play around with aphrodisiac. Obviously, the most common is chocolate; however, there are numerous others less obvious options to choose from that can help bring out that dormant sexual desire that you are looking to release from your partner. Incorporate these aphrodisiacs into snacks, deserts and meals.

(4) Pamper her with a seductive massage

No woman in her right mind is going to turn down a massage. As such, you offer your woman a massage; just incorporate some seemingly innocent and subtle actions into the massage that can get her attention and/or raise her desire to have sex. Whether you let your hands 'do the walking' on her body or you gently put the print of your lips on her neck as you rub the tension out of her shoulders, adding a seductive element to a massage is a sure bet to get her love juices flowing.

Five Tips to Start Dirty Talking

Be original

You don't want to sound rehearsed and you don't want to sound too practiced. Also, you don't want to sound like you studied this and you don't want to say something that doesn't pertain to your man. Say something that is for him and only him. It will make it a unique and special experience for both of you that way.

Be confident

This may be the biggest tip of them all. If you are not confidence, he will be able to tell and it will come across as awkward and weird. Don't make this happen. Be sure about what you are going to say and believe it.

Keep it at bay

When things are heating up, it can be easy to take things a little too far. Keep the reigns on and make sure that they stay at a certain level. Don't get ahead of yourself or rush things!

Have fun

If you aren't enjoying it, he will be able to tell. Make sure that you are having fun and letting loose with dirty talk. It's supposed to be fun!

Be yourself

Men might not be the sharpest knives in the drawer at times, nor pick up on what our subtitles are all about, but he can tell when you are not being yourself.

At the end of it all, you just want dirty talk to be fun. It shouldn't be something that you feel pressured into doing nor something that you aren't comfortable or confident with. If you ever feel any moment of hesitation or discomfort, your man will pick up on it and he will feel awkward.

Here's a good rule of thumb to keep in mind:

"If it sounds bad in your head, don't say it out loud."

If you are trying too hard to come up with something to say, then it is going to sound unnatural and rehearsed. Instead, try to say things that come up in the moment. This is when you are at your most authentic and this is when you are going to be at your sexiest for him.

Remember to have fun and to enjoy it! Dirty talk is fun and it is something that can seriously amp up your bedroom play and become something special between the two of you

Romance Tips For Your Girl

Guys! You are now dating that hot girl. How do you keep her? Love and dating advice made easy.

1: Start slow

The best way to keep a girl's attention is to inform her that you want to go slow. Wait until the 4th date to have sex. Some dates should just be cuddle dates.

Women are so used to men just wanting them for sex, that only cuddling is a great way of getting close and holding her interest. Not to mention raising her anticipation levels for the big event.

2: The perfect first kiss
A very light brush is better than a full on tongue kiss. First of all, it gets her curious and wanting more. Keep something back for later.

3: Compliment her
Most women are very insecure about the way they look. Women look at their imaginary physical flaws (butt too big, flabby thighs, whatever) and find it hard to believe that a man could find them sexually attractive. Constantly tell her how sexy you find her. If you can improve her self-esteem she will be much more uninhibited in bed.

4: Planning
It's easy to get caught up in work and before you know it the day, or week, has passed. Use your organizer as a reminder to phone your girl unexpectedly. Girls love a quick call or text to say "hi, thinking of you".

5: Public Dirty Talking
Whispering, explicitly, what you would like to do in a more private venue makes it more likely to happen. This is because sex talk in public is doubly arousing. The anticipation and naughtiness will have her all hot and bothered in no time.

6: Some 'her' time
Arrange for her to go to a beauty salon, spa, or hair place. Tell her you are going to dinner after. When you collect her, take her to a restaurant attached to a romantic hotel. She will be feeling fantastic after her beauty treatments and all of these romantic gestures will totally overwhelm her. A sure fire way for a little romance.

7: Fireplaces
All girls love romantic getaways involving fireplaces. Cozy cabins or rooms, big rugs on the floor, dim lighting, mulled wine or champagne and no sports on the television, all add to the romantic ambience. A great way to spend a winter's day.

8: Cherish her completely

All women have a little secret something about themselves that they are proud of. This normally does not involve a body part. It might be her black sense of humour or her individuality. You need to find this, and love and appreciate this. This is when she will feel loved as a whole person and then you will have her sexually and emotionally. No idea what's going on inside her head? Is there anything her father compliments her on that lights her up?

9: The necktie

This clothing item is the favourite of all women. Take it off and use your imagination.

10: Makeup sex

Anger while fighting drives up the testosterone in both of you. Increased testosterone means a stronger sex drive. If you haven't been fighting, try a pillow fight or naked wrestling in the bed, to get things heated and breathless.

11: Gifts

All women love unexpected gifts. Show her you understand her by making it personal. Try for thoughtful and creative. The timing of the gifts appearance could be crucial in how the evening turns out.

12: Take her shopping

Buying a new outfit puts girls in the mood for romance. Having her guy with her in the mall makes her happy. Make sure that if you are going to go that you stay interested. Do not be half hearted and do not wander off and get lost. Apparently, in Victoria's Secret lingerie stores there are love seats in the dressing rooms. Do you need any more incentive than this to go to the mall?

13: Kiss her more often

The most common complaint from women is that their guy does not kiss them enough. You should kiss your girl for more than 5 minutes while you are whipping off her clothes. Women like to be kissed through the whole encounter. Women love being kissed everywhere. Find her favourite places to be kissed and make sure you include them every time. Nuzzling, licking and soft nipping are usually appreciated as well. This sort of strategy will decrease the amount of headaches she will have.

14: Say it. The top 3 romantic things women love to hear from men are:

"I just love waking up with you."

"I have brought you a little something"

"I can't wait to see you"

15: Listen
To keep your romance alive you need to listen to her properly. Here is how:

Turn off the television. Yes, off, not just on mute.

Listen to her.

Repeat what she has said.

Tell her that it makes sense or clarify if you do not understand.

Turn television back on. Better yet, give her a cuddle.

16: Make a fantasy box
Both of you get to write down your own secret sexual fantasies. Fold them over and place in your fantasy box. When you want to spice it up, pull one out for inspiration.

17: Never buy carnations
Carnations are cheap. They come over as cheap and from the corner store. You will never impress her with these. They will never be seen as a romantic gift. Save your money for something else.

18: Make her breakfast in bed
If you can't cook, a cup of coffee and something in the toaster is still a great romantic idea.

19: Never Hesitate
"Does my butt look big in this?" Never, ever hesitate. The only correct answer is "No."

Follow this with a cuddle with your hands running appreciatively over her curves for a more genuine feeling response.

20: Be her friend
You have to concentrate on the friendship side of the relationship, not just the sexual side. The more you understand her thoughts, the more she will reward you.

To have a hot wild date needs a little romance. Dating and romance just need a little thought and planning. These romance tips will keep your dream girl coming back for more.

Bed Dirty Talking

If you are looking for new ways to please your man in bed, you may want to explore and learn how to talk dirty in bed. Indeed, nasty talks during lovemaking can turn on your man and can intensify the sensations that you both are feeling at that moment.

In fact, many women love to hear dirty talks as well as it will stimulate your imagination and help you focus on the sexual act at that moment. Talking dirty may even help women in forgetting about other things running in her mind as well.

If you want to talk dirty in bed, you have to keep in mind some general rules and caveats when doing the dirty talks. Remember that dirty talks can arouse or can turn off your partner, depending on how you do it, and remember to practice.

If you are naturally a little noisy in bed, you may not find it difficult to talk dirty in bed, but if you are the silent type, you may want to practice before pulling off the stunt in the wrong way.

- Practice to talk sexy. Your voice is a big factor in making your dirty talks effective. In fact, men are said to enjoy a sexy voice during lovemaking as that turns them on. Of course, they love to hear moans and responses from the woman as well, as these are signs that the woman enjoyed the act as much as he does and he was able to satisfy her.

- Pick the right words to say. Yes, you can voice out your dirtiest thoughts about making love but make sure you are also using words that can arouse your man and not turn him off or make him laugh. Forget about those technical and medical terms. Find and research nasty words that are more appropriate for dirty talk. There are a lot of resources that can teach you how to talk dirty in bed and you can practice saying those words in bed as well.

- Start slow. Do not surprise your man with nasty talks. He may be startled that you have uttered such words that he'd never heard from you before. If you are a beginner, you can start slow with moans and then slowly introduce some nasty words little by little. You don't have to recite every dirty word you have learned from the magazine. Take your time and slowly introduce dirty talk into your lovemaking.

- Give your man an ego boost with your dirty talks. This will also give him more pleasure by letting him know that he turns you on or he is hard to resist. It also turns them on to know that women enjoyed and are satisfied with their sexual prowess as well.

- Identify the right timing. Of course, learning to talk dirty in bed can be effective if you are able to explore your sexy voice, if you have the right words chosen and of course, if you tell it to your man at the right timing.

Maximize Pleasure From Dirty Talking

There can be so many pleasures that come from dirty talking with your partner, it is something that you can both enjoy, explore and certainly have fun with. There are downsides though, you can't get too distracted in dirty talking to your partner that you're not actually enjoying the experiences yourself. So although dirty talking with your partner can be fun and exciting in your relationship.

You need to make sure that you don't get too distracted the best way to do this is by verbalizing what is currently going on at the moment. Don't get too hung up and try to hard on trying to sound like a porn star or as if you're reading an erotic story. Thinking about dirty talking to much can sometimes ruin what is going on and that is the last thing that either of you want from it. So instead of putting a lot of pressure on it and making everything perfect and sexy, it can be done very easy if you just talking and tell your partner what you're thinking or feeling. If you're thinking about him doing something that you particularly like then tell your partner.

An example of this is if you caressing or massaging your partner tell them how much you like how something feels or ask them if they like it when you do something certain, whispering in your partner's ear is a great way of telling them what you want or what you like if you're not feeling amazingly confident. Telling your partner what you're going to do next is also is a great way of giving your partner something to get excited about or possibly to prepare themselves for! The great thing about dirty talking like this is the anticipation of what's about to happen will work them into a frenzy and make will have them wanting more.

Another good thing is to use your own voice to request things that you want your partner to do or say. Everyone wants to please their partner in bed and give them a pleasurable sex life, so using dirty talking as a way of asking for something and giving some direction may be just the thing they want to hear.

They can't guess what it is you want them to do so being a little assertive and telling them, still dirty talking to them though can be a big advantage to the both of you. So don't be shy about asking for what you want when you are dirty talking with your partner.

Praising is another great technique when it comes to dirty talking, telling your partner that when he or she touches you that they're doing something well or you like something that they are touching in a certain way. There are so many ways you can praise your partner that will boost their ego and their arousal. Make sure not to take it too far and being patronizing to them, saying "You're doing a great job" is not the same as telling them how much they're turning you on and could go down the wrong way.

Naughty Sex

I want you to take a few seconds toimagine the following scenario:

You come in from a hard day's work and as soon as you get through your front door, your woman gives you a HUGE SMILE and looks really pleased to see you. You smile back, take her hand, pull her in close and give her a big kiss and a cuddle.

She makes dinner (whatever your favourite food is) and you share some conversation and a little wine (or a couple of beers) with your food. Then you relax for half an hour on the sofa - either listening to some music or watching television. Next, things get interesting...

You look at her and she looks at you and she takes your hand and demands that you take her to the bedroom. So... being the cool guy that you are (who is always willing and able to SATISFY HIS WOMAN) you take her to the bedroom and have sex with her. But you don't just have any old sex - no, no, no... you have really dirty, really naughty sex. You have the kind of sex that every man wants (but not many men ever get).

You get all the BLOW JOBS you could want and your woman even WANTS you to give her ANAL SEX. And remember - this happens every night (not just once a week or once a month like it is for many couples). Sounds pretty good, right?

Now, what if I told you that there is a way to make the scenario I described for you above a REALITY? Would you like to know how to do that? I thought you would. So pay close attention, because what I'm about to share with you has the power to take your SEXUAL RELATIONSHIPS to the next level.

Naughty Sex - How To Make Your Woman Give You Everything You Want In Bed (Blow Jobs Included)

In order to get EVERYTHING you could ever dream of in the bedroom, the secret is actually very simple. Here it is...

Give Your Woman Amazing Sex.

Seriously, when you give your woman amazing sex - she will willingly do pretty much ANYTHING you want in the bedroom. Give her great sex and all the blow jobs you could ever dream of will be yours. You'll also be much more likely to get her to want ANAL SEX and even group sex (if that's your thing).

Now, let me tell you how to give your woman amazing sex... First, you must know that amazing sex is not giving your woman one clitoral orgasm using your tongue or fingers. You can give her an ORGASM that way - but that is not amazing sex (it's just OK sex).

Amazing sex is the kind of sex that causes your woman to brag to her friends about how good you are. Amazing sex is the kind of sex that makes your woman think of you as "the best she's ever had". And to give your woman amazing sex, you must give her many types of orgasm. Give her clitoral orgasms, VAGINAL orgasms and MULTIPLE orgasms.

Give her orgasms so hard and so powerful they bring a tear to her eye. Give her orgasms that make her scream your name so loudly it wakes the neighbours. Basically, give her sexual pleasure like very few men know how to give a woman. Do that and she will be eternally grateful, meaning that all the BLOW JOBS and other naughty things that you want from your woman in the bedroom, will become yours. Guaranteed.

In order to give your woman great sex and lots of ORGASMS, you must do several things that the "average man" does not do. For starters, you must respect your woman outside of the bedroom. Only when you respect your woman will she fully open up to you and surrender to you in the bedroom.

Next, you must always tell the truth and be a man of your word. This builds TRUST. Once you have a basic level of trust, you can then go on to build SEXUAL TRUST with your woman. Without sexual trust your woman will never get really naughty with you in the bedroom.

So if you want all the blow jobs and anal sex you could ever imagine - never lie or be dishonest with your woman.

INSIDE THE BEDROOM you must take control and lead your woman. Women are sexually submissive and they like strong, sexually confident, manly men. When you become that kind of guy and take control of your woman, she will love you for it.

Please remember that you must only TAKE CONTROL inside the bedroom. Your woman does not want you to control her outside of the bedroom. In fact, men who try to control their women outside of the bedroom are the exact opposite of what women want. They are weak, needy and insecure.

To give your woman great sex you must also TALK DIRTY. Women love dirty talk because it stimulates their mind (and for women, sex is very mental). Many men are afraid to talk dirty, but you must "step up" and use your voice in the bedroom if you want to become "the best your woman has ever had".

There is no other option. Other things you must do to give your woman great sex are to use techniques like The Welcomed Method and The Deep Spot Method to give her orgasms like no man will have done before.

And also remember to do things differently each time you have sex with your woman. Make love to her in many ways and in many locations - otherwise things will get boring. And if you allow the sex to get boring - your woman will stop wanting it. I'll finish by giving you two powerful examples from my own personal life.

With my first girlfriend (before I really worked out what great sex was) I had the kind of frustrating sex life that many men have and perhaps that you have right now. I wanted more sex than my girlfriend and I didn't know why. What's important to note is that at that moment in time I thought that giving her one clitoral orgasm each time we had sex was enough. How wrong was I!

Anyway, I split up with her and met a new girl. This time things were very different. I educated myself and I gave this girl incredible pleasure. I gave her clitoral orgasms, vaginal orgasms and multiple orgasms EVERY TIME we had sex. I also sometimes gave her squirting orgasms and even orgasms with no touching.

Now, let me ask you a few questions...

- How many blow jobs do you think I had with this girl?

That's right... as many as I wanted.

- Do you think I had anal sex with this girl?

You bet I did.

- And do you think this girl wanted as much sex as I did?

Truth be told - sometimes she wanted MORE THAN I DID.

Now I think you'll agree that is a massive contrast between those two relationships. And all I did to make the change was some learning. I taught myself how to give women incredible sex. It wasn't easy, but it was worth it.

After-all, a man's greatest pleasure is pleasing his woman. Are you pleasing your woman?

Benefits of Dirty Talking

Talking dirty during the sexual activity help to lose inhibitions and to be more "unconscious" during the sexual act. When we reach orgasm, the brain releases oxytocin, a hormone that reduces stress and lowers the risk of depression. And when we are more relaxed, we are also more likely to say what we like under the sheets. We don't worry if what we say is out of place or if our moans sound like the sounds of a dying dog. Free from anxiety, we only think about reaching the pinnacle of pleasure and, for this, we are more open-minded.

They increase the excitement and intensify the experience of the relationship.

They allow you to take control ... or lose it, depending on your taste: using dirty language during sex helps to establish the roles that the two lovers assume and to understand better what you want. Telling, driving, dominating...They help women to overcome the "good girl" complex, that sort of prejudice for which a woman must be good and quiet, otherwise she will never be a good wife and her reputation will be ruined.

Women let you go: Saying bad words in bed will make you feel free to express your sexuality, satisfy your desires and feel good about yourself, without trapping yourself in the categories of 'slut' or 'bride'. Speech is a tool that denotes a certain independence. Free yourself from all these labels.

Last but not least, they allow us to free ourselves from taboos and feed our sexual fantasies, creating new ones. Talking dirty therefore becomes an opportunity to reveal our dark sides and experience things we would not normally do. "Insulting" your partner is not really thinking what you say, but simply putting one of these fantasies into action through language.

In summary, this practice can be very useful to dissolve or "break free". Some of us suffer from educational or religious beliefs, and sometimes in bed they may have trouble expressing themselves as they would like. Of course, this can happen like a game, in cases of deeper closure: erotic themed jokes are fine, as well as laughter with certain vulgar words that we will never pronounce in other contexts.

Moreover, dirty talk can be useful to explore one's sexuality and express, even as a joke, your fantasies to the partner. Which in fact can also lead to their realization, if you wish. Do not overlook the fact that the intimacy of the couple could also benefit. But even for this practice, rules are needed.

3 Golden "Rules" To Not Exaggerate
1. Always be in agreement
Consensuality is fundamental in any area of sex. Discuss with your partner first to see if dirty talk is something you can practice or one side doesn't like. For some people, silence is golden.

2. Set Your Stakes

Although it is not a practice that is part of the BDSM, you can think of agreeing on a safety word for dirty talk too, to avoid going too far. In general, however, it is good to agree with your partner on what you can and cannot talk about, what kind of language to use or what fantasies to use.

It means that for you, as a couple, this practice is not taboo in itself, but you need rules. Much better than jumping without a parachute into an experience that can be extremely unpleasant for some.

3. No insults

It can happen that, in a moment of passion, you let yourself go and say something inappropriate. It can be understood, it can be justified. But transcending the rules of behavior could be one of those stakes we mentioned.

Insults - especially of a sexist nature - can be intolerable even in **these contexts.**

Dirty Talk to Woman

Have you at any point had dirty considerations about a young lady? Have you at any point needed to advise her precisely what you need to do to her until she's hot and sweat-soaked and prepared to hook your garments off?

All things considered, if I know most men, you've likely kept those considerations and words to yourself. You may have even retained them while you were connecting with a young lady for dread that she may get outraged and leave. However, try to keep your hat on; she's hanging tight for you to break out the dirty talk. So I'll talk about properly dirty talk with ladies and take your and her experience to the next level.

I stared at her for a minute. Her eyes darted and began to dance around the room, but I directed her gaze downward as an escape from my fascination.

We discussed some mundane topics, but the words were evaporating into cloudiness of vitality and trade of vibes. Yet, the subtext trade couldn't have been clearer. Her students started to extend, and her palms were getting sweat-soaked.

I snatched the rear of her head and pulled her toward me until my lips were inches from her ear. I realized she could feel my hot breath stinging the side of her face. I started kneading her scalp. I began to talk from my stomach, guaranteeing my voice was, in any event, an octave lower than typical. I seized a tight her other arm. I revealed to her that if we weren't in an open scene, I would punch her in a bad position, pull her hair back and kiss her everything over her neck while I ripped her garments off. Also, before the night finished, she realized that I was a long way from all talk. And keeping in mind that I was strolling the walk, I kept on dirtying conversation with her until she wanted to discharge the creature inside.

I've had a ton of involvement in dirty talk when connecting with young ladies or sexting them. Maybe to an extreme, some could state. Yet, I can let you know no ifs, ands, or buts is that ladies love sex, ladies love dirty talk.

However, such a significant number of men are just hesitant to push the sexual envelope. They are worried about the possibility that the lady will get awkward, or she will dismiss them, or they will become uncomfortable because they are wandering into a new area. In any case, in light of your faltering, I will share one of my preferred Mark Twain cites:

"Quite a while from now you will be increasingly disillusioned by the things that you didn't do than by the ones you did. So lose the anchor. Sail away from the sheltered harbor. Catch the exchange winds your sails. Investigate. Dream. Find."

If you've perused my pieces previously, you've heard me talk about my dread of "imagine a scenario where?" Cultivating this dread is how I had the option to wreck approach tension. Getting dismissed, extinguished, missing the mark... everything can be highly excruciating (until you, in the end, understand that you're realizing, that is), however nothing. I amount to nothing, and it is more agonizing than lament. Realizing that as a man, you could've accomplished something; you could've acted, yet you didn't do anything.

So sail away from your protected harbor and take a risk for once in your life. You have no clue how a lot of a young lady will regard you. What's more, you might be astounded at the outcome. Also, in particular: do it for yourself.

Fortunately for you, dirty talk is anything but difficult to learn and a great spot to begin if you need to start stretching the limits more.

Stage 1: *BE A SEXY MAN*

If you're attempting to dirty talk to a lady, you've never laid down with, or hell, a lady you haven't had more than one discussion with, the possibility can be overwhelming. It very well may be not very comforting just to consider it. The truth of the matter is, when most men attempt to dirty talk to ladies, they appear to be:

Unpleasant

Clumsy

Uncaring

Excessively Aggressive

In any case, they fall off in these ways for reasons that you may not think. It's positively not because ladies don't care for dirty talk. Instead, they should prepare for dirty talk.

If you put on a show of being excessively forceful: This implies you didn't appropriately set up a young lady to get sexual. It is primarily a problem for men who are dark-skinned.

If he is perceived as too forceful or engaging in dirty talk, he will be directly in line with that recognition, sending her into auto-rejection. To truly connect with a young lady, you must first get her in the right frame of mind.

If you put on a show of being obtuse: This implies you shifted the state of mind to sexual when there was excessive "well disposed" of a vibe, or if you were profound plunging her and she was trusting in you. If a young lady is disclosing to you a genuine anecdote about how she lost her dearest youth little dog and you begin talking about how you need to get her bare, she'll feel like you're attempting to utilize her.

If you put on a show of being clumsy: This implies you set an awful point of reference with the young lady, and your being sexual just left the blue. Or on the other hand, it means that you haven't gathered up enough social speed, and you're conveying uncomfortable vibes.

If you put on a show of being dreadful: This implies your non-verbal communication is clumsy, you haven't developed enough social confirmation in her eyes, you didn't give her plausible deniability, and additionally, your style/game is excessively powerless.

Usually, I wouldn't say I like to praise silver projectiles, but on this occasion, I can say that you can fix these visual cues by doing something: improving and adjusting your provocative vibe.

121

Suppose you're perceived as being overly forceful. In that case, your provocative vibe is powerful, and you need to dial it back with more energy and make her giggle/feel quiet to open herself up to your advances further.

If you're experiencing being unbalanced or frightening, your attractive vibe is excessively frail. You have to take a shot at hitting young ladies with your provocativeness directly off the bat. You are putting on a show of being overly "safe," and a young lady doesn't consider you to be a darling natural alternative.

If you're experiencing being inhumane, your provocative vibe is confounded. You have to associate with the young lady on an enthusiastic level and cause her to feel like she's interfacing with you. And afterward, you can alleviate the strain with a joke or some light prodding and begin to get sexual.

Stage 2: *SUBTLE DIRTY TALK EARLY IN AN INTERACTION*

Except if a young lady is already warmed up and ready, you'll need to start the dirty talk in a light and subtle tone. I was as of late bantering to and from with a young lady. We talked about work and snickering about entertaining proficient stories – nothing too naughty... until I tossed some unobtrusive sexuality in with the general mishmash. I quit snickering, took a gander at her as though I needed to get her, and to maul kiss her at that moment. Then I got a slight grin all over.

Me: But that is only my regular everyday employment. You couldn't deal with what I do around evening time...

Her: [a sultry look in her eye] Oh definitely... and what might that be?

Me: I'm a janitor. Because I get dirty, I make things wet, and I deeply inspire individuals.

Furthermore, this line (and lines like these) did an astonishing thing for me. It was an explicitly charged line, so it made her go and in an increasingly sexual outlook. Be that as it may, after I said it, she wanted to chuckle because it's only a clever line too. So it deals with two levels. First, great inconspicuous sexuality imparts sexual subtext while keeping the outside layer of correspondence light and fun. Since she's giggling, she can't blame you for being unpleasant or excessively sexual; however, since you did offer a sexual remark, she sees you more in the sweetheart casing. Sexual jokes, when utilized well, can be advantageous assets for pushing cooperation ahead.

Stage 3: *ESCALATE TOUCH*

If you've been taking part in light sexual chitchat, this is an ideal opportunity to begin contacting her. You ought to be energetically getting her while you exchange, and as you start to profound jump her and make the connection more substantive, you should begin utilizing the more delayed types of touch.

Stage 4: *TURN UP THE HEAT*

If you've built up an association with her, turn up the sexual warmth when she least anticipates it. Don't do it if she's revealed to you a genuinely charged story and is searching for your approval, yet do it when you are talking about yearnings like travel, or are kidding around to alleviate the strain, or are simply examining a progressively unremarkable theme. For instance:

Her: And that was the insane story of my excursion to Bali!

You: Wow, that was a powerful story! I'm going to call up National Geographic at present! Also, after all that, here we are in an arbitrary American jump bar. Isn't this the fantasy?

Her: Haha, I know, right... this is life!...

You: [grabbing her arm, and inclining indirectly by her ear] Sarah, I need you to know, if we weren't right now, be kissing all over your neck at present, sliding my hands down your body and grasping a firm your hips. Also, I'd be beginning...

And afterward, you pull back, staring at her for a second, and later, keep talking regularly. And after that, propose setting off to a calmer spot or getting a nightcap or setting off to an after gathering, or whatever else goes to your head.

Short note: if it's truly on, you don't need to return to the ordinary discussion. You can disclose to her that you folks can get it going and leave at that moment. So this should be founded on your judgment.

Stage 5: *THE AMAZING "NO SEX" LINE*

I took in this line from a characteristic companion of mine. When I initially began utilizing it, its viability bewildered me. Furthermore, all the more stunning was that the more smoking the young lady was, the better the line became.

So it goes this way: while you're on the stroll back to your place or her place – or if it's a lesson when you show up at your goal – you stop the young lady and get a natural look all over. Then you look her dead in her eyes and summon up each ounce of sexuality that you have in your body.

We should make one thing straight...

Young ladies are sexual animals. Young ladies love sex. Young ladies consider sex, possibly more than you do. Young ladies, ladies, anything you desire to allude to the more pleasant sex as – they are not these unadulterated, chastised animals numerous in the media describe them.

I trust you knew this, yet I needed to ensure we agreed. What's more, since you know this, you ought to likewise realize that each young lady appreciates a touch of sexting now and then, mainly while she's ovulating. It's science.

Why You're Getting No Sexts

If you're perusing this article and thinking, "Gee, I wonder why I never get any sexts from young ladies?" then you've gone to the perfect spot. You're not getting any sexts because you're presumably doing one of a couple of things wrong.

Issue 1: *Attraction Type*

You may not be making enough fascination. Not the "Goodness, he's charming and perhaps I'll let him take me on a couple of dates" sort of fascination. I'm talking the "oh crap! For what reason am I following this outsider into his condo" some kind of sexual fascination.

If she's not explicitly into you, you most likely won't get any sexts, exposed pictures, or dirty talking from her. Instead, you need to stir her to get filthy writings and photographs from a young lady. You can't simply pull in her. She needs to effectively consider your rooster somewhere inside her before she'll effectively draw in you in sexting. Furthermore, unmistakably, this is simpler after you've laid down with a young lady...

Issue 2: *No Sex for You*

You may not be getting sufficiently laid. It's constantly more uncomplicated to get stripped pictures and dirty writings from young ladies you've laid down with previously. You'll generally be playing a daunting task if you're attempting to get things warmed up before laying down with her. It's conceivable, however, more complex.

Issue 3: *Tactless Thirsty Dudes*

You should know how to talk dirty with her appropriately. Instead, you go from "0 to 100" way too rapidly. Rather than preheating the broiler, you're excessively ravenous (or parched). You toss it in on sear and afterward overlook the stove miss when attempting to take it out. You have no tolerance or class.

Ladies love men of activity. They love men who follow what they need, done in the best possible way. Continuously be a man of honor. You shouldn't ever appear to be an audacious or inconsiderate social retard with no channel.

For instance, this is terrible content to send to a young lady:

"Decent gathering you the previous evening, can hardly wait to f**k you sideways in the not-so-distant future."

There is no trade. There is no such thing as a tease. There isn't any sizzle. You appear to be thirsty.

This young lady will lose the fascination she had for you, if any whatsoever. She will think you think she is a prostitute and disregard you.

The most effective method to Talk Dirty to Girls Over Text (and ideally get some provocative shots)

Cautioning: The accompanying sexting models are very immediate, and we would prefer not to appear hostile. We accept that a man ought to endeavor to be however much gentlemanlike as could be expected and approach each lady with deference and profound respect. In any case when it goes to the room, indeed, isn't tied in with getting dirty?

Here you go:

Be Playful and Tactful, But Slow Down Until You Know Her

Presently we talked about being parched and utilizing class to get her heated up. Everything is situational, and once you know a young lady, you can pull off significantly more than with a young lady you don't know excessively well.

There is a scarcely discernible difference with a gradually done idea. You, despite everything, need to be the energizing sort of man she'll be content with. In this way, you need to be prudent, however energetic simultaneously truly.

For instance, with a young lady you had pretty recently met the previous evening or a day or two ago, you could begin a discussion off explicitly with something like this:

"Great to meet you the previous evening... that provocative minimal bum of your is going through my head... completing no work today; you're a horrible impact on me!"

This model is fun-loving, and she'll appreciate the tease. You'll likewise certainly disclose to her you're a sexual man, not some pleasant, exhausting fellow – the sort of fellow she's presumably exhausted with.

You can genuinely begin things rapidly. This is a genuine case of a quick conversation with a young lady you've already gotten physically involved with:

You: "Well, it's Thursday evening, I'm off work, and I'm so horny when I consider you... what can I do?"ha

Her: "Get some ice?"

You: "Senseless young lady, that is mischievous. You weren't honored with hips like that to no end... get the decent clothing, some red lipstick, and get here at this point!"

This young lady will come over and go through an exquisite night ass exposed with you, as long as she doesn't have any too squeezing plans. You were reckless, however diverting. You caused her to feel hot and overwhelmed. You didn't put on a show of being a wet blanket. It means by which you dirty content.

Start From the Beginning

Presently, the ideal approach to begin a dirty messaging discussion is to start from the earliest starting point. Be that as it may, you can't be an awkward wet blanket in doing as such. You can begin a discussion with a, to some degree, sexual vibe. It is because many folks abstain from being lively and sexual for the most part.

Start with the light wicked stuff and prop up from the absolute first content. Then consistently attempt to transform things into a sexual insinuation, regardless of whether it's cheesy. You don't need to talk about twisting her over a work area in the senior member's office to stimulate her.

For instance:

Her: "Hello you, how's your day going?"

You: "Gracious hello gingersnap... a touch of exhausting to be straightforward. Need some fervor today... "

Her: "Really? What sort of energy :)"

You: "Idk, perhaps an agreeable house cleaner who's does all that I ask... "

Keep the vibe fun and coy from here. You can keep sexting, or you can push for a meetup.

You May Offend Her

You will, in the long run, annoy her. Or, on the other hand, one of your "hers" will get irritated. You will be dirty messaging, and she will get resentful. This is fine. Don't be a colossal bitch and start saying 'sorry' in a needy way. Mellow outplay things cool. She may simply be trying you.

In any case, you have to give a slight expression of remorse. One approach to do as such:

Her: "that was extremely discourteous"

You: "Ahhhh I didn't offend you really awful, did I? Ugghhh fine, you get one punish and that is it... "

You acknowledge and recognize her annoyance, but you refuse to submit to her will. She, despite everything, regards you, and you've kept up her fascination.

Jumping Deep – Dirty Texting for Experts

If you're a virgin and like to remain as such, you won't have any desire to keep understanding this. Notwithstanding, if you're prepared to take your sexting to the following level – read on.

Here are a couple of increasingly master dirty messaging tips:

Running The Questions Game Over Text

You should, as of now, be running "the inquiries game" on pretty much every first date. It's the most straightforward approach to plunge into more profound subjects and take a sexual discussion. Young ladies love that poop.

It's additionally a simple method to take a messaging discussion to a sexting discussion. Here's the specific system you should utilize:

You: "so wanna play a game."

Her: "Umm, sure."

127

You: "Cool inquiries game. Three inquiries each, yet you need to answer sincerely. No falsehoods or BS. You can't rehash the inquiry another person previously posed."

Her: "Haha, alright, however you ask first."

You: "I'm a man of honor. Women consistently start things out."

Presently a dominant part of the time, she'll battle you on this. That is fine. You can contend somewhat to and from. She may ask first, or she may "make" you.

If she asks first, answer every one of her inquiries genuinely and give her criticism if they are exhausting. If they are sexual, you're set. If she gives you exhausting ones (and is a held young lady) and you reply, you then mirror her inquiries while including a touch of edge. When she answers, give criticism and afterward cycle two. She may start to sexualize, or she may not. When you find a workable pace second round, you do.

If she "makes" you ask first, you can turn it on her rapidly:

You: "Well, I was going to get along, yet since you're in effect so obstinate..."

Try not to hang tight for her reaction:

You: "1. What number of men have placed their rocket into your pocket?"

You: "2. Do you like being commanded in bed?

You: "3. What's the one sexual thing you've for the longest time been itching to attempt yet never had the nerve to do?"

These are the cash questions. You need to find a workable pace in the game. They are what is important. So – regardless of if she goes first, you go; first, the vibe isn't sexual...

You need to find a workable pace. She might be shy; however, she'll reply. Flippantly get down on her about anything that doesn't sound genuine. Spitball a piece on her answers, then state

You: "Your turn."

She'll ask you, in any event, a couple of sexual inquiries, generally every one of the three. The answer truly, yet offer to warn her if anything is "as well" odd or insane before advising her (model: you've had 200 sexual accomplices).

Run one progressively adjust and pose two sexual inquiries dependent on her answers (model: What turns you on the most? How would you generally come?). Toss in an investigation dependent on her youth too. You need it to be sexual yet light. Something like:

You: Did you ever find a good pace greatest pound in middle school?

She'll reply. After two rounds, you ought to have enough things to be content about. First, let the inquiries game part of the sexting vanish.

In the wake of making her warm-up, you can request nudes if you think all is good and well.

Messaging Her to Orgasm

You can utilize this after the inquiries game or in a different circumstance. For example, if you have a young lady who is sexual from the hop, a young lady you've laid down with previously, or a young lady with whom you've appropriately raised the convo, you can calmly offer to walk her through a climax.

When she's somewhat worked up, from some sexting, you can say:

You: If you ask pleasantly, I may let you have a climax.

Her: Umm, not certain what you're talking about, however sure

You: Say please and evacuate your jeans.

Her: Ok and please

You: Good young lady. Presently envision I'm there...

You: over you. I've nailed you down against the bed. I'm going to take you while you squirm and groan in delight. You feel a shiver between your legs as my hand contacts you. I get a clenched hand brimming with your hair and pull you close before kissing you profoundly. My fingers go through your hair as we kiss.

You: Then I get you and through your hands behind your back and curve you over. SMACK. You feel my hand gives your rear-end a firm smack. You whence as you groan. You feel a sting, however a lovely sentiment as well. So I take my belt and limit your options together.

Her: gracious wow

You: you need more?

Her: yesses

You: I push your face into the pad and pull my hand back to punish you once more... this time hard. You howl in torment; however, the cushion suppresses your groans. I instruct you to quiet down and take it like a decent young lady.

You: I flip you over and push you on your knees. I stand up and look at you without flinching before making you suck my hard chicken as I stand. You take my hard cockerel in my mouth as I powerfully get your hair. I begin to push a more significant amount of my chicken in your mouth as you choke.

Her: ahhh, this is acceptable.

You get the idea, folks.

You simply keep messaging her dirty until she says she intends to come. Then tell her you haven't let her in yet. After a few more sex texts, you conclude with:

You: "Cum. Presently."

The key is to warm her up before finding a good pace, reveal to her you'll make her come. When she's warm, be extremely unequivocal and prevailing in your writings. Then don't let her come until after the peak of your sexual story. That is when you utilize the last content.

Don't hesitate to request naked photographs, mainly if she came.

Requesting Photos, The Right Way

A few young ladies will send you photographs unexpectedly. A few young ladies will never send pictures. A few young ladies will send photos to folks they've engaged in sexual relations with. A few young ladies will spam photographs to everyone.

If you've warmed her up through content, you are in a situation to request photographs. When she's warmed, you can pull off pretty much anything as long as you don't send "nudes" or something weak like that.

In any case, possibly you've engaged in sexual relations with a young lady yet haven't been sexting a lot. It would be best if you got nude photographs of her; however, you might not have the opportunity to put resources into a lot of sexting. In addition, she's not the sort to send nudes for reasons unknown or unexpectedly.

Whenever you shag her, offer it to her great multiple times and be harsh with her. Ensure you finish a piece sweat-soaked and exhausted. As you spend, you'll need to turn over and tap your chest. She'll move her head on your chest, and you'll cuddle a piece.

Please give her a light kiss on the temple and gradually recapture your breath. Then commendation whatever piece of her body you need photographs of, yet state it in an exasperated way:

You: "God, you have a decent screwing ass."

Or then again...

You: "Fuck, your tits are great."

You then slap her rear end and get her tit. Delicately, you would prefer not to intrude on the post-coital cuddles.

What's more, recall – the commendation must be veritable.

She won't overlook it, mainly if you screwed her right.

Presently, you may discover she sends you a photograph of her rear end as well as tits inside seven days of this event (once more, contingent upon how well you screwed her). If she doesn't, you have set yourself up to request a bare.

Start a discussion. It very well may be ordinary, yet ensure things are somewhat perky, then bring it up:

You: "For reasons unknown, that bum of yours won't leave my brain. It's screwing tormenting me. I can't rest. I can't eat ;)."

Her: "Haha, that is not my shortcoming. You're the wicked kid ;)."

You: Ahh, well, I can't deny that; however, I do know a pic or three of that bum may help with the entire eating and resting."

She may not send them immediately, yet she will in the end because you asked pleasantly.

One key thing to recollect: if you've found a workable pace in discussion with a young lady, you can and often should stack these dirty messaging tips. For instance, you can begin by running the inquiries game to sexualize the discussion. Then the idea to walk her through a climax. When she finishes, you could demand a couple of nude photographs as a much obliged.

Dirty Talk to Man

Today you will figure out how to talk dirty to your man to make him rock-hard for you.

Regardless of whether you are right now single, in a long-haul relationship, or even wedded, you should know a few deceives on the most proficient method to pull in a person and keep the sentiment and the science between both of you alive.

Realizing how to talk provocative and dirty to your man, sharpening those abilities to flawlessness, and later really applying them in your affection life can be both animating and energizing.

Attractive dirty lines as an incredible asset

Attractive dirty lines, when utilized accurately, can assist you in withdrawing a person like a moth to a fire. Nonetheless, if you don't know what you're doing, the entire thing can reverse discharge and flop hopelessly.

There is no requirement for me to dive into insights concerning your sexuality and attractive dirty talk. It serves just to engage you to relinquish your limitations and ultimately make the most of your sexuality on your standing.

What better way to communicate and investigate the boundaries of your sexuality than figure out how to talk dirty to your sweetheart?

You don't have to worry because I'll tell you exactly how to talk dirty to your man right now. Vital prescience about people before you gain proficiency with the craft of dirty talking. Before you start learning how to talk explicitly to a man, you should consider the two people.

Sonnet by Victor Hugo - "Man and Woman"

"... Man is the flying bird.

She is the songbird that sings.

Flying is a predominant space. Sing is to vanquish the spirit.

The man is a Temple.

The lady is the Tabernacle.

Before the sanctuary we find ourselves, we stoop before the Tabernacle.

In short: the man is set where the land closes.

The lady where paradise starts."

Acing True Sexual Pleasure with the Help of Dirty Talking

According to Dr. Ava Cadell, a proficient speaker essayist and sex advisor in Los Angeles, couples engage in dirty talk to "increase their excitement and offer dreams that they may not want to transform into the real world, but talking about them can be shockingly better."

Sex in combination with the ideal and energetic sweetheart leads to consistent sexual delight and unadulterated rapture.

Following that way will take you to find and understand the genuine significance behind sexual joy and love. It will clarify your brain and contemplations.

Also, dirty talk is perhaps the ideal approach to upgrade your sexual delight and satisfy your sexual dreams.

Today you'll find and completely ace the specialty of lovemaking and sexual delight with the assistance of dirty talk.

I need you to make each stride right now talk manage gradually and consistently to handle the central idea of talking dirty to a man.

When you nail this center concept, you'll present yourself with a whole new and increasingly significant level of sexual and mental fulfillment in your relationship.

The purposes behind learning and applying these dirty lines

Remember that perusing and utilizing the dirty talk lines won't just set you up for sexual joy but also your man's endless and future love and warmth for quite a while.

Rehearsing these systems and adhering to the guidelines on talking dirty to him, you will immediately turn into the ace of the ideal lovemaking, leading you to the spots you have never been and taking your relationship to another level.

Consolidating extreme and energetic love with compelling and prevailing sexual joy will make your relationship a lot more grounded and stable.

Utilizing the attractive expressions from this article will turn your sweetheart on and cause him to hunger for you more than ever.

Get to know his sexual inclinations

An examination led by the internet dating office, Saucy Dates, has uncovered that both, types of people, love commotions and words during sex.

So for this dirty talk to do something unique for your sweetheart, you should initially get to know his sexual inclinations instead of talking dirty to him right away.

Answer the inquiries.

Just by noting a few straightforward yet powerful inquiries, you will have the option to comprehend and discover his different preferences during sex. Those inquiries are the accompanying ones:

Does he like to be predominant when it comes to sex?

Does he act forcefully, harshly, and like your proprietor?

Does he lean toward being agreeable?

Does he utilize antagonistic language and angry or debilitating reactions?

Which body some portion of yours stands out for him the most?

Is it safe to say that incredible entertainers and fundamental characters firmly pull him in?

Do famous people he's pulled in to have the equivalent or comparable highlights?

A discreet and straightforward young lady nearby, a wild lady with solid sexual nearness, or honest?

The most effective method to Combine His Sexual Fantasies with Dirty Talk to Blow His Mind

Finding out pretty much all the sexual dreams he's shared, which are the most widely recognized topics he prefers, and what are his most shrouded wants?

Is it to be revered like a lord, associated with an undertaking, or rule a solid and influential lady?

Has he at any point had the accompanying sexual dream?

A case of the most well-known sexual dream:

The silk scarf tied around my wrists was cutting into my skin. Even though the blindfold was closing out all of the light, I, despite everything, had my eyes shut. An unexpected sharp spot of my left areola made me howl in delightful torment.

"Shhhh, Baby, you aren't permitted to make clamor. Do it again, and I will beat you!" he said. I pondered opposing him. . . to savor the smack of his hand against my rear end. However, before I could open my mouth and state something, I felt the tickle of a plume running up my internal thigh, and afterward, our lips squeezed together in an enthusiastic kiss.

Unexpectedly, he stops and pulls away. I am feeling lost and bewildered, not realizing where he'd gone. In any case, this was all piece of the game. He was halting and beginning. Hard and delicate. Torment and delight.

My faculties were alarmed and honed, not realizing what was in store straightaway. He could tell I was restless, so he consoled me. "I love watching you so turned on and needing me.

Gesture your head if you need me at present." I needed to be fantastic; however, I shook my head enthusiastically and began shouting yes. I was unable to see it, yet I swear I could feel his grin broadening. "Presently spread your legs as wide as could be expected under the circumstances so I can embed my penis. Hold them like that until I reveal to you that you can move" All I could do was to comply.

I was naked. My arms and legs were attached to the bed. I was bare with my legs spread as much as I could.

Defenseless. Terrified. . . be that as it may, I consented at any rate. Furthermore, that was exciting and energizing.

In this way, enough with the sneak peeks!

If you are ready, how about we get familiar with the expressions that drive men wild and talk dirty.

1. *Coquettish (and marginally dirty expressions) known as consideration grabbers*

It is ideal to begin simple and utilize basic and coy expressions on your man. Simply dunk your toes in the water to perceive how sending a dirty instant message works out for both of you and whether it will get the need you need.

Have a go at sending something like this:

1. Stop. . .

- diverting me

- turning me on, I can't focus

- filling my psyche with wicked considerations

- pondering me. Return to work

2. Mmmm...

- I am thinking some extremely yummy things about you at the present time

- I continue thinking about your astonishing kisses

- you are terribly adorable, you realize that?

3. Are you. . .

- reddening? You ought to be, founded on what I'm thinking.

- rested up? I intend to deplete you on Saturday.

- turned on as, am I? Stunning.

4. Damn...

- contemplations of you make them grin today

- I am so turned on by you

- I can hardly wait to be sleeping with you

5. Know what?

- I can hardly wait to feel your kisses.

- You are one hot beau.

- I just escaped the shower. Appreciate that visual.

6. Can I simply let you know. . .

- your arms are damn hot

- you have me turned on

- how great you looked an evening or two ago?

7. Disclose to me something. . .

• do we look great together for sure?

Content him these dirty lines to consume his brain until whenever he sees you (make them consider you)

1. What might you do. . .

• if you were here the present moment?

• if I was there with you?

• if we were separated from everyone else at the present time?

2. I can't quit pondering. . .

• how my body reacts to your touch.

• the things I need to do to you.

• the things I need you to do to me.

• the entirety of the spots I could kiss you.

3. Envision this. . .

• me running my fingers through your hair as we kiss and you getting so rock hard down there.

• me snacking your neck and gradually working my mouth down your body

• you are contacting my delicate skin, investigating my neck. . . shoulders. . . back. . .

4. I can hardly wait to. . .

• feel your body by mine, skin to skin. . .

• jump on you when I see you!

• have you in my bed, alone, and continuous. . .

• make you my attractive love slave

• run my hands over every last trace of you and make you cum.

His answers may inspire a scope of feelings and sexual strain. After perusing your messages, he will stir and prepare for you immediately.

Be that as it may, if things gain out of power at the very beginning, don't stress; you don't need to partake if you think it is unreasonably best in class for you.

You can generally utilize some cooling sex expressions, for example,

• Whoa there! We should spare some for some other time.

You can utilize any line of the accompanying:

• Oh you are so shrewd.

• Slow down sir, a lot of time for those exercises.

• I have you truly turned on huh? Shrewd me.

And afterward, separate yourself from him, saying you need to come back to work, meet your companions or make sense of another motivation to walk out on him. Anything that will put a halt to the discussion.

He won't realize what hit him and conceivably respond peculiarly and unexpectedly. If, in some way, his response is genuine and sweet, then try to keep things at a PG-13 level for the time being.

2. *Sext-starter – The best dirty talking lines to use on your sweetheart*

The most ideal approach to begin the discussion is with a lively sex talk message that asks for his reaction. Something that will make his creative mind go out of control:

• If you were here. . .

• I wish. . .

• Guess what I'm doing. . .

• Stop. . .

• Know what?

• You have me soooo. . .

The ellipsis utilized after the expression won't just keep him fascinated and curious about what follows straightaway yet additionally let him know there is something else entirely to the idea.

Your dirty and unusual content will assuredly confound him; however, over the long haul, he will know he's in for a treat.

What he can anticipate from you when he gets such a dirty provocative message is a sizzling sex shock.

The sext-starter will make his creative mind go crazy.

From that point forward, you can control the discussion any bearing you wish by talking explicitly to your man.

You can attempt to hop immediately by sending him sexting "fast in and out" or start gradually and progressively advancing into his heart and bother him into talking explicitly with you.

Here is the means by which you can dirty provocative talk to your man.

3. *Sexting Quickie – Hot and Steamy Messages*

When you have assembled some involvement with talking dirty to your man, you can utilize something nastier, and at last unusual, so the accompanying lines are perfect for you:

1. If you were here. . .

- I'd stroke your hard chicken and imploring you to screw me.

- I'd be face down, ass up on the bed so you could top me off so profound.

- you'd make the most of my tight, wet kitty feline. purrrrrr. Mmm...

- my pussy is so prepared for you, infant

- I need to fold my mouth over your rooster at this moment

2. You have me sooo. . .

- horny at this moment. I need you to screw me terrible.

- turned on and wet, omg I need to feel you inside me, screwing me hard.

4. Fun loving and Innocent Sexy Texts

If you aren't happy with the nastier stuff, then you can generally return to fun, energetic and honest approaches to content your beau.

1. If you were here. . .

- I would meet you at the entryway absolutely exposed.

- I wouldn't have the option to keep my hands off of you.

- you'd see exactly how wicked I'm in the state of mind to be. Extremely underhanded.

2. I wish. . .

- I could feel the heaviness of your body over mine at this moment

- you could feel precisely how turned on I am at this moment

- you and what's in your jeans were before me this second.

3. Mmmm...

- do you have any thought how turned on I am by you?

- the considerations I'm having at the present time. Is it true that you are reddening? You ought to be...

- I am aching for your touch right currently child

And afterward, when you have made a casual air, you can take swift, decisive action by sending him nastier messages as:

If you were here. . .

- I would take you in my mouth, licking and sucking until you lose control.

- you could twist me over the rear of the lounge chair and take me. . . rigid. . . the subsequent you stroll in the entryway.

- you could pour nectar all down my stripped body and lick it allllll off. . . inch by inch.

2. Stop. . .

- making me so horny. I can't complete any work considering what I need you to do with my body.

- filling my head with delightfully dirty thoughts (then proceed to depict).

3. You have me sooo. . .

- turned on. I need you within me, topping me off, making me groan sooo terrible at the present time.

- wet at the present time.

5. Clear and direct messages for dirty provocative talking

Being transparent and direct will get you to place you need. Sending these profoundly enticing dirty provocative writings will hit the dead center.

Be direct and let him precisely know what you need him to do to you OR what you need to do to him.

Take a stab at sending something along the lines of:

- I can hardly wait for you to... in my...

- I can hardly wait for you to gradually disrobe me taking a gander at me with your attractive room eyes.

- I can hardly wait for you to snack my areolas. Licking, sucking, a touch of gnawing. Do you realize how hot that gets me?

- I can hardly wait for you to give me your hard chicken in my eager pussy.

- Tonight I'm heading off to... your... until you...

- Tonight I'm going to stroke you with my hot wet tongue until you go over the edge with delight.

- Tonight I'm going to suck your chicken until you cum.

- Tonight I'm going to ride you until you cum so hard infant.

- I need you to... my... until I'm...

- I need you to lick my clit until I'm squirming and groaning and peaking.

- I need you to screw me from behind until I'm making such a lot of clamors, I wake the neighbors.

- I need you to go down on me until all aspects of my body is shaking with delight.

- First, I'm going to... Then I need you to...

- First, I'm going to torment you with a moderate, provocative strip bother.

- Then, when you can't control yourself for one increasingly second, I need you to have your way with me.

- First, I will jump on my knees, unfasten your jeans, and bring you profound into my mouth. Then I need you to look as I do something amazing until you detonate.

• First, I will slather whipped cream all over my tits. Then I need you to take as much time as necessary as you lick everything off.

These are only a couple of essential recipes that make it simple for you to begin.

Also, as should be evident from the models, sometimes you need to change them somewhat, so they bode well for the specific bearing you are giving.

As you become agreeable, by all methods, release your inventiveness and work out your own unequivocally specific writings!

Dirty Talk Games

Women LOVE SEX! They want to be teased, seduced, satisfied, and pleased! Jump start her sex libido tonight with 4 tips to share some exciting sex games with her! You better write down how she is right now because you won't believe the difference. Try it tonight!

1st Tip. How To Prepare Her For Sex Games.

First of all, most men don't realize that women really love fantasies and sexual games. They also crave more attention, excitement, and communication. A sexual game with lots of fantasies satisfies all these women's needs. So you don't have to do much in the way of cajoling your lady to take part...if you approach it right.

Don't force her to do anything. Just ask her about her fantasies and let her imagination take over. Her imagination is huge and could dwarf yours.

Once you find out the type of fantasy that turns her on then just ride with it. Satisfy her long-time fantasy and of course she will want to be a part of it. What woman wouldn't?

2nd Tip. How To Pick A Sex Game.

There are many sexual games that you can invent yourself. Therefore, they are totally FREE. I'll just give you some successful principles to make your own.

Maybe you just need a few ideas to get started. Obviously, if it doesn't take much money to get into the game then that will help lots of couples with this economy.

Make sure the game doesn't offend either of the participants in terms of their religion, morality, and so on. Why start off on the wrong path?

Make sure that your agree on the risk level. Don't force her to do something that scares her too much.

The easiest way to pick the sex adventure is to have the woman share her fantasy and then you jointly pick one that meets her expectations.

Just talking about it will draw you closer together as a couple and help to turn her on. She may even have a no-touch orgasm by getting involved!

3rd Tip. How To Fully Enjoy It.

Once you have made your plan then follow through on it. Don't put it off. Take a dry run on it by talking her through the steps. Again, this may turn her on so much that you quit talking and have some fun! There's nothing wrong with that!

Cast your abandons to the wind. Check everything out and plan every detail. Then just go for it! Risk is part of the adventure as long as it is calculated risk!

4th Tip. Hot To Multiply Your Enjoyment Thereafter.

You could decide to video your encounter. Then you can enjoy it thereafter. Also, this now sets the standard for what you can do in the future. You can have many pleasant (and hot) moments rehearsing what happened.

She could also enjoy some residual orgasms where she plays today and enjoys great climaxes days later - even without touch! Take advantage of that free fun!

Start today and have your great adventure. Remember, the more combinations of fantasies, games, and techniques will determine your excitement level.

Good sex is great, but is "good enough" sex really good enough? Often people who have been sexually involved with each other for a long period of time may find that their sex lives fall into a little bit of a rut - it's fine, but it could be better sex. And the same can be true for some couples who are just starting out; there may be a little something missing, perhaps because they feel a little shy or unsure of themselves. Assuming penis health or another problem is not an issue, there's no reason that such couples shouldn't be enjoying even better

143

sex - and one way to help achieve that goal could be to incorporate sex games into bedtime activities.

Sex games are a fun way to add a little spice back into sex play or to help "break the ice" among those still getting to know each other. There are dozens of games out there that a couple can use in search of better sex. Here are a few that they can consider to get themselves started:

- Strip anything. Almost everyone knows about strip poker, in which people play cards but instead of betting with money, they bet with pieces of clothing. But the fact is that there are numerous other games that can incorporate stripping. For example, get a pair of dice and have each person pick a number - say, five for him, eight for her. Roll the dice. Every time a five comes up, he takes off a piece of clothing and the same for her when eight is rolled. Or to make it more fun, let her take off his piece of clothing when five is rolled and he take off hers when eight is rolled.

- Distracted wooden tower. Take one of those stackable wooden towers and put it together. As with normal play, the trick is to remove pieces of the tower without it falling down. The challenge in this version is that as the player is trying to remove the piece, their partner is rubbing and massaging their genitals to distract them.

- Penis ring toss. The man picks out five sex positions and assigns each one a number, without letting the partner know what they are. He then stands with a firmly erect penis while the partner tosses five plastic hoops, trying to get them to land on his penis. If, say, three end up around the penis, they then have sex using whatever position was assigned the number three.

- Orgasm race. The partners masturbate each other, trying to make the other reach orgasm first. Vibrators and other sex toys may be used. Determine an appropriate prize for whoever wins - whether it's sexual, like getting to determine what sex position to use the next time they have sex or practical, like taking out the garbage.

- Sexy slips. Each partner takes several slips of paper and writes on each one of them something sexy he wants the other to do, e.g. "Tie me up with stockings" or "Service me orally at the breakfast table" or "Masturbate in front of me." Each partner draws a slip and has to follow the instructions. (If they are unwilling or unable to, they can pass - but they should talk about why they are reluctant to do it.)

Sex games are one route to better sex - but the best route involves being willing and able to communicate lovingly and openly (if tactfully) with a partner.

Dirty Talk Examples

Some of the best dirty talk examples of companionate love can be found right here. This type of love is intimacy without passion and is more-intimate than friendship but only when the presence of commitment exists. A good example for this type of love is a level of love that is most commonly found in marriages.

Although the passion may be gone there is still a deep and undying affection or strong liking and a commitment to those that are loyal to their vowels. This is not an ideal situation for any marriage but marriages can and still do survive in this environment.

A good example for talking dirty for a companionate type of love is; I need you tonight inside me. While this is not over-the-top it is extremely direct and straight-forward and is really the message that a physical action is desired.

There does happen to be a situation were a companionate love can grow into the most desired form of love which is consummate love. Although this is not a rare occasion there still exists a smaller percentage of this type of escalation of love, unfortunately for most couples. It seems as if in the world today companionate love, when in motion, the majority of the time seems to fall back to empty love and then liking or friendship.

Once the bar has been lowered to a friendship level of marriage this union normally does not have a chance for survival unless it is a marriage of convenience. If this is a case dirty talks can really help by initiating a reversal of fortune and maybe going back up to companionate love.

The bottom line is that love is a many splendid thing but talking dirty can add spice to any level of love. One of the best ways to look at a list of best dirty talk examples is an actual list! Please have a look at the phrases and terms below that were created in hopes to reiterate a favorable response either in the bedroom or even on the phone.

Love making is a very special thing indeed and with spicy talks and naughty utterings you may just break open that introverted lover that needed just a little push. Please have look at the list below and see if any of these dirty talking examples is something that you can try on your lover tonight.

Best Dirty Talk Examples Listing

* Give it to me Hard

* I'm your Little ***** Tonight

Do you notice all the absence of vulgarity? How can you make even the most innocent dirty talk phrases a bit more romantically inclined? By using body language to really bring home the point! If it is your intention to elicit an eruption of emotion from your lover tonight then please do try one of the examples listed above. Believe in what you are saying as a lie painted and wrapped up in a flowery expression of love is never a good thing. Your partner deserves your loyal and honest and ethical answers and behaviors and this is what a truly consummate love is all about.

1. If we weren't here (insert public place) right now, you'd have absolutely no chance of keeping your clothes on.

2. Do you think I have panties on right now?

3. What are you doing after work, I need some of your cock ASAP.

4. Damn, you smell good enough to eat.

5. I just want to make you whole face wet with my juices.

6. Are you hungry baby? I want to swallow you up.

7. If you keep looking at me that way, I'm not responsible for what happens to your cock.

8. I can't stop thinking of what you did to me last night.

9. I need your body near me right now. Get over here.

10. I can only think of one thing right now, and it's you naked in my bed.

11. Do any of these people around us right now have any idea what a stud lover you are? (Let's keep it our little secret.)

12. I can't imagine sharing you with anyone, you're so freaking hot.

13. Why don't you suck on my peaches, they're plump.

14. Do you want to suck on my nipples while I fondle you?

15. No one needs to know that your hand is up my skirt right now.

16. Can I touch it?

17. You make me so horny, I can't stand it.

18. Just looking at you makes me wet.

19. I'd like to share every inch of my body with you.

20. I'm ecstatic just thinking about your cock every day.

21. When I wake up in the morning, the first thing I think of is how you fuck me.

22. I haven't seen you in so long, but I can still remember your body like it was yesterday.

23. Let's fuck in front of a big mirror so I can see you making love to me.

24. Why can't I have you right now? None of these people need to know.

25. I like licking your stick.

26. When you pull my hair, it makes me want to come.

27. I want you all the way inside me, give me all of you.

28. Your cock is so delicious.

29. Why can't I have you like this all the time, you're my new addiction.

30. Your body feels like heaven. I'm insatiable.

31. This cock is all I need, and maybe some air.

32. Your dick is so full. It feels amazing.

33. When you hold my buttocks that way, It makes me explode.

34. What naught little thing do you want me to do to you next?

35. You have no idea what you've gotten yourself into. I'm going to be your sex slave.

36. Yes, that's what I like. That is so hot. Fuck me more.

37. Fuck me more I'm going to cum.

38. I want to make you come so hard.

39. Let's fuck again. I want more.

40. I'm going to wear you out.

41. Let me get on top of your cock, sweetie.

42. You need to grab my tits and hold them while I cum.

43. You're so naughty.

44. I'm your naughty girl.

45. Your cock is huge.

46. I want it inside of me as soon as possible.

47. Fuck me now, I can't wait.

48. How do you want me to fuck you? Like this?

49. Slow and easy, or fast and crazy. I'll fuck you however you like.

50. Do you want to watch me suck you?

51. I love when you're hard.

52. Stop being such a walking turn on.

53. I wish you could be inside me forever.

54. You make me so wet it doesn't feel real.

55. Why do you drive me so crazy?

56. God you turn me on so much it's not fair.

57. Stop being so delicious.

58. You are giving me an oral fixation.

59. I wish I could eat you for breakfast.

60. You drive me crazy.

61. You are so hot it is wild.

62. You're driving me crazy... in the best way.

63. You are the biggest turn on.

64. I'd give the world to fuck you all night long.

65. You are so hard, now I want to feel you connected to me, I want your cock inside me right now.

66. You touching my body drives me crazy, the feel of the touch of your fingers, your lips and your tongue is amazing.

67. I feel so hot and wet.

68. I am so horny right now.

69. You feel amazing inside me.

70. I feel so good and so alive right now.

71. Pass your finger over my lips.

72. C'mon, I want you to undress me.

73. Hmmm, yes, you are doing it right, please don't stop, keep going.

74. I want to feel you inside me right now, give it to me baby.

75. That little thing you do with your tongue inside me, it's insane.

76. How can I please you? Can I suck on you a little?

77. Do you want to dive inside? I'm nice and wet for you.

78. I can't stop thinking about what you did with your dick the last time we were together. It's magic.

79. How do you do the things you do in bed? You make me all wet and bothered.

80. I have no powers of concentration right now. All I can think of us sitting on top of your hard cock.

81. I want you to fuck me from behind next time.

82. What is your fantasy? What should we try next? I'd like to fuck you in the shower.

83. No matter how far you are, I can feel your dick inside me.

84. I'm not wearing anything under this robe, and I'm touching myself thinking of you.

85. What do you want me to do to your cock when I see it again?

86. You have the hottest ass I've ever seen.

87. I want you to look into my eyes while you penetrate me deeply.

88. How fast do you want to come?

89. I've been thinking of how perfectly you fit inside of me.

90. Remember that time that you fucked me against the wall?

91. I can still taste your dick on my lips.

92. I can't get enough of your cock. It's like my food.

93. It's official, I've been dickmatized.

94. I want your cock and no one else's.

95. My pussy is just for you.

96. I'd love to sit on you all day long.

97. I love how you taste/smell. I could get drunk off of your juices/scent so easily.

98. I love the sounds you make

99. You sound so sexy when I'm going down on you

100. I want to fuck you until I can feel that sweet little pussy clenching around my cock

101. I want you to cum so hard that I feel your cock pulsing inside of me

102. I'm really looking forward to seeing you tonight. I think we should have some fun ;)"

103. You should probably already have your pants off when I get home... I'm feeling playful."

104. Baby, I'm really horny. What do you want me to wear for our date tonight?"

105. I had the sexiest dream about us last night... and it gave me some inspiration for our date night next weekend ;)"

106. I've got a sexy surprise waiting for you tonight..."

107. I'm having a really hard time focusing at work today... can't stop thinking about what we did on our date last night ;)"

108. (With a sexy photo already prepared) "I just got out of the shower... want to see?

109. (If you don't live with your significant other) "What are you doing later tonight? Mind if I stop by to blow you/go down on you? I'm really craving your cock/pussy in my mouth right now.

110. (With a sexy photo already prepared) "I'm touching myself right now thinking about what we did last night... want to see a photo I just took for you?

111. Mmm... I still feel deliciously sore from last night. You certainly know how to show a lady/guy a good time.

112. I definitely just came thinking about you riding me

113. So turned on thinking about _____. I'm about to take matters into my own hands...

114. – That feels amazing baby

115. Come sit on my lap, love

116. Mmm... do you like that?

117. I need you right now

118. Just lie back and let me take care of you

119. I'm getting so turned on/wet/hard

120. Tell me what you like/if this is too hard/when you're about to come

121. You look so beautiful/handsome/gorgeous/manly right now

122. What do you feel like doing to me?

123. I love how your hands feel on me

124. I love when you talk to me like that

125. I love when you grab me like that

126. I love when you look at me like that

127. I love it when you growl

128. You are so sexy

129. Ughhh... I love your body so much

130. I feel so sexy when I'm in your arms

131. I love how you look at me when you're turned on

132. You can have me any way you want me baby

133. Mmm... I can tell that you're having fun

134. Where do you want to cum?

135. You feel so good inside of me baby

136. I want you inside of me

137. I want you to tease me until I can't take it any longer

138. I could spend all day between your legs

139. I love feeling you this deep inside of me

140. I can't wait to taste you on my lips

141. Mmm... you taste so good baby.

142. Your beautiful body feels so good in my hands baby

143. Are you ready for me to enter you?

144. I love what you're doing to me right now

145. I'm getting close

146. I love it when I can feel you squeeze your pussy around me

147. I want you to cum for me

148. I want you to cum all over me

149. I want you to cum inside of me

150. You're going to forget your name after I'm done fucking you tonight

151. (When you like something that they've done/they're doing) Mmmmm... good girl

152. Relax... just lie back and let me make you cum

153. I want to dominate you tonight

154. Your cock fits in me so perfectly

155. You have a very talented little mouth

156. You have such a perfect little pussy... I love it so much

157. You have such a perfect/gorgeous cock... I love it so much

158. I want you to dominate me tonight

159. (Taking her hand and putting it over her vagina) Show me how you touch yourself baby... I want to see you surrendering into your deepest pleasure for me

160. Mmm... I fucking love it when you ride me like this

161. Get on your knees, now

162. Is this pussy yours? Are you going to take it?

163. You look like a sexy little angel with your lips wrapped around me like this

164. I love sucking your cock so much

165. Pound my little pussy with your big cock daddy

166. I'm going to drain every last ounce of cum out of you

167. Tell me how much you love it when I fuck you/when you fuck me

168. I want you to fuck me in front of the mirror baby

169. Do whatever you want with me daddy

170. I want you to be as loud as you can when you cum

171. You have such a perfect ass/cock/pussy/body/etc.

172. You're a good little slut, aren't you?

173. Ask for permission before you cum... I want to hear you beg for it

174. You look so fucking sexy right now

175. Cum in my mouth. I want to taste you.

176. Mmm... good girl. I want you to cum for me, hard.

177. Tell me how badly you want me to fuck you

178. Show me how wet you are my little slut

179. I want you to fuck me until we wake up the neighbours

180. Stand up and fuck me

181. Fuck me harder!

182. Yeah daddy, give me every last drop of your delicious cum

183. I love it when you grind that little clit on me

184. Use me like your little fuck toy

185. I own this pretty little pussy

186. I want you to gag on my cock/fuck my face

187. Ride me harder

188. Keep that pretty little mouth open to me when I'm fucking it

189. I love sucking your cock daddy

190. I'm your whore

191. Yeah, ruin my pussy. Take it!

191. What a well behaved little whore you are

192. You own me

193. Mmmmm... yeah, fuck my face

194. That pretty little face deserves to get fucked

195. Don't make a sound until I tell you to... and if you do, I'm going to pause and wait until you can be quiet again, like a good little boy/girl

196. You're going to need crutches when I'm done fucking you

197. Tell me who owns this fucking pussy

198. Fuck me daddy. Don't stop!

199. There is something so damn hot when you pin me down by my wrists.

200. Hearing you groan, moan and shout when you cum is so fucking satisfying.

Conclusion

It is fundamental to establish ground rules with your companion. Many people, as previously said, are afraid of seeming ridiculous or being laughed at if they speak dirty. It's critical to establish ground rules, such as not criticizing or laughing at each other, or correcting each other's attempts to speak dirtyly. It's crucial to feel safe while trying out new things.

KAMASUTRA

What Is Kama Sutra

Everybody knows Kamasutra, the book of sex and love. Let's see where and when this text was written, as well as what its genuine meaning is.

"It is desire that makes things happen for lovers joined in sexual pleasure [...] In the war of sex, lovers, blinded by passion and overwhelmed by impulsive energy, do not pay heed to the hazards [...]." This passage is from Chapter 12 of the Kamasutra, an old Indian text full of advice on eros, love, and sexuality.

Inside, the optimum postures to hold during intercourse are depicted in order to reach "kama," which signifies pleasure or ecstasy in Sanskrit. Let us attempt to learn more about this book, its author, and its significance.

Meaning of Kama Sutra

The Kamasutra is an ancient Indian treatise about sexual activity. It is a significant piece of Sanskrit literature that deals with love, desire, pleasure, excitement, sensuality, and sexuality.

Vatsyayana wrote Kamasutra in the second century, and the full title of the book is Vatsyayana Kama Sutra, or "Aphorisms about Vatsyayana's Love."

The Kamasutra is a collection of seven works that describe how to establish human harmony. According to the author, every man must have four goals in life: happiness, pleasure, ethical sense, and freedom from the material world. Of course, the most well-known section is the one on pleasure, which the author claims may be accomplished in 64 various ways, referred to as arts. There are eight distinct methods to make love, each divided into eight positions, for a total of 64 possible ways to make love. Each position is depicted with graphics and is usually denoted by an animal's name. The part of the book dedicated to sexual positions begins by addressing the subject of kissing, then deepening on topics such as foreplay, orgasm, oral sex, and even threesomes.

In Indian culture, in fact, sex is a form of divine union that has nothing to do with the idea of a sinful act that has spread to the western world.

The complete work, therefore, addresses moral issues, deals with courtship and relations between men and women. In particular, the first book talks about the relationship between man and woman; the second focuses on kissing, foreplay, sex; the third is based on courtship; the fourth on the behavior that a wife must have; the fifth summarizes the art of seduction; the sixth deals with the topic of courtesans, while the seventh chapter explains how to revive a passion that has now gone out.

The History Behind Kamasutra

Legend has it that the Kamasutra was conceived by the Indian god Shiva, who, having discovered the pleasure and joy of sexuality with her, fell in love with the female projection of himself. He wanted to immortalize his sexual habits, dictating them to the servant Nadin, and this encounter was very totalizing.

Over the years, before the final version published by Mallnaga Vatsayayana, the text (aimed exclusively at the rich because the poor could not read) was then revised and expanded by many. The Kamasutra is composed of 7 books in its final edition, edited by Mallnaga Vatsayayana around the third century AD, aimed at describing how the relationship achieves human harmony. The first full translation of the Kamasutra in the West dates back to 1883, a time of complete British supremacy in India, and was by Richard Francis Burton of England. The Kamasutra, unlike the Tantras, is not a holy text, and its reading does not require a guru's guidance. There is no reference to Tantrism in the text itself, for which it is sometimes mistaken. The primary aim of Kamasutra is to teach men and women how to act to ensure a happy love life in the face of sexual desire.

The Social Ramifications Of The Kama Sutra

When Vatsyayana first penned the text that we today know as the Kama Sutra, he could have had no idea of the economic impact he was creating. A manuscript brought to life by a man who history has all but lost has created such legal issues through the course of history as to make it one of the most highly debated and vilified texts in publication. Let's take a few moments to reflect on the social ramifications of the Kama Sutra on Victorian culture in Great Britain.

From A Publishing Standpoint

From the publishers standpoint, the ancient Sanskrit text has been a glowing success. This is easily evidenced by the many translators who have took upon themselves, the task of rewriting and compiling the manuscript for the masses to enjoy. The first such translator for the English language was Sir Richard F. Burton, a British explorer who spoke no less than twenty-five languages fluently. When he discovered the text upon one of his journeys of exploration through India in 1842, he became enamored by the book and decided he must translate the text into the language of his peers back in Great Britain so that they too could enjoy the material he was now so fond of. Thirty-four years later, in 1876, Sir Richard Burton had finally finished the work of translating the

Kama Sutra with the assistance of his collaborator, Forster Fitzgerald Arbuthnot, since Sir Burton could not read ancient Sanskrit himself. The first published tomes were still a long way off however.

The Kama Shastra Society

Seven years later, in 1883, the first English copies of the Kama Sutra were published. That first edition consisted of 250 privately published copies of the great manuscript. These copies were published by The Kama Shastra Society, of which Burton himself was a founder. The Kama Shastra Society was created to keep Burton and his peers from being prosecuted and imprisoned by the Society for the Suppression of Vice under the Obscene Publications Act of 1857 and was used by Burton as a method of publishing much of his work over the years. If the society had not been founded, his many endeavors in the field of writing and translation would have been set to the wayside by popular Victorian society of the time, as Burton, himself, was considered to be less than savory by his peers. His translation and writing often dealt with subjects of a erotic or highly sexual nature which was very counter-culture to the Victorian society of the day.

Some of his works that would otherwise be lost to the world today included a translation of The Book of a Thousand Nights and One Night (Most commonly referred to as The Arabian Nights and considered to be pornography at the time due to sexual content.)and a translation of the Arabic guide called The Perfumed Garden. Sir Richard Burton had written a second translation of the same work which he titled The Scented Garden but this was tragically lost along with several other papers when his widowed wife, Isabel, burned them after his death in October of 1890 from a heart attack. The irony of her destructive action is that Sir Burton had intended this translation to be published after his death as a way of providing for his widow through the proceeds.

The Kama Shastra Society provided for a private publication and distribution of the Kama Sutra to its own member thus circumventing the Obscene Publications Act of 1857 because they could not be prosecuted for sharing a private Society publication amongst its own members. It is interesting to note that Sir Burton's work did not become legal in Great Britain until the year 1963, eighty years after its first publication and seventy- three years after Burton's death. What is even more interesting is that a text with absolutely no illustrations was considered so offensive to the British censors.

The Benefits of Kamasutra

It invigorates a connection.

Long-term spouses sometimes find that their relationship becomes stale with time. Experimenting with various positions may spice up a couple. Some classes, such as the Corkscrew and the Carousel, encourage closeness.

It improves a person's sexual pleasure.

Kamasutra isn't only about sex. It considers sex to be more than simply a physical experience. It is a method of achieving fulfillment through pushing one's physical limits. Sex energises the body while also enhancing the immune system? Overall, Kamasutra places a high importance on the sex experience since it allows partners to feel good about themselves both physically and intellectually.

While experience and physical strength can help determine how delightful and practical more advanced sexual positions are, there is one technique for everyone to get physically prepared to try them out. This is also sound advise for folks concerned about their flexibility or having difficulty entering more accessible sexual positions:

Take a yoga class or any other type of exercise that focuses on stretching and strengthening your core muscles. The stronger a person's core muscles are, the better they will be in holding various physical positions and have higher overall physical endurance. The more limber and flexible a person is, the simpler it is to move into and maintain difficult positions.

Additional Practices and Steps to Spice Up Your Sex Life

Some people attempt making love or even starting their foreplay with pornography playing in the background to spice up their sex life. Some couples may begin watching pornography together to increase arousal, while others like to have it on as a guide during foreplay. This approach is not for everyone, but it is a great strategy to attempt if you want to learn more about your spouse's sexual preferences or want to visually convey your sexual preferences to your partner in a thrilling and engaging way.

Another option for couples who wish to improve their sex life is to begin their sexual activities before ever sharing a room. Text messaging and the ability to exchange photographs with cellphones has made this far more convenient than it was in previous decades when technology was inadequate. This method does need some amount of confidence between partners, especially if images, video, or audio recordings are to be shared from one phone to another.

The goal of this game is to get the most out of your foreplay. Some couples begin sending each other filthy text messages as soon as they leave for work in the morning, gradually increasing their sensuality and seductiveness until both parties are ready for physical foreplay and intercourse nearly as soon as they get home that evening. When trying this activity, some safety and security tips for men and women are:

Avoid putting your face in any pictures or videos; do not mention names or specific locations in audio recordings; and do not save any pictures or videos that you or your partner would not want someone accidentally stumbling across or finding if your phone is ever stolen.

If you don't want to get in trouble, don't open video or audio communications at work or in public.

While some people may enjoy the risk (it's possible that the risk is one of the reasons the couple chose this method), if anything were to open unexpectedly or be taken by virtual hackers who could be used against the couple, the dangers would shift from exciting and entertaining to very real and unfortunate.

Advice from an Expert for Couples of All Ages

Never use a dry spell as an excuse to call it quits on a relationship. Intimacy is complicated, relationships are complicated, and there are many elements that can affect someone's ability to become aroused:

Emotional, hormonal, psychological, social, and physical stress are all factors to consider.

Dry spells are common, especially among couples who have been together for a long time. While a medical difficulty is always a possibility, for people who have been cleared by a doctor for concerns with their personal sex life, the remedy can be as simple as altering the routine and trying something new. Any of the concepts, strategies, or activities discussed in this book can be utilized to rekindle a sexual passion (in yourself or your partner).

Other possibilities include going to a sexual supplies store or exploring the internet for sex guidance. Every day, new stores and galleries open to cater to people's sexual desires all over the world, regardless of how weird or unique their inclinations may be. Whatever sexual preferences you and your partner have, it is up to both of you to come to terms and communicate properly in order for your sexual, emotional, and romantic interactions to succeed and be completely satisfying!

The Kama Sutra Sex Positions

Sex is not cut and dried. A lot of different sexual positions are set out by the Kama Sutra. Going down the list, we will go through various sexual positions that not only give you sexual pleasure but also bring you and your partner on a deep, intimate level closer together. The positions we are going to go over are the following:

Standing Positions

The Fan

Standing, with her knees tight on the edges of a chair and her arms crossed on the back, the woman gives her back to the partner who first brings her to him by insinuating her hands between her slightly spread thighs to stimulate her

clitoris, then penetrates her from behind. This position - suitable for both anal and vaginal coitus - allows excellent stress on the woman's vaginal walls and G-spot. Man can also caress her clitoris or breasts before and during penetration.

The Padlock

On the table, on the desk, on the washing machine: the position of the padlock is versatile and guarantees magnetic contact between the two bodies ... The woman is on a high cabinet (a desk, a table, the washing machine), sitting cross-legged and resting on the arms, positioned behind. The man stands in front of her, and the woman crosses her legs behind him, at her sides. He stares at her as the movement begins.

Luxurious Climb
The couple stands face to face next to the bed. She puts one leg over the bed while the man kneels until he can put her leg over his shoulder. She hugs him around the neck so she can relax and let herself go backwards as the man slowly gets up to penetrate her. She stretches her leg and stretches it to the maximum while he continues with his constant movements.

The Royal Stairs
The woman kneels on the lowest step of the staircase and leans on an upper step or on the railing. The man takes her by the hips and penetrates her from behind. This position can also be used for anal sex.

Standing on a wall

The man has his back against the wall and penetrates the partner holding her by the thighs and moving the pelvis back and forth to modulate the oscillation of the back and forth.

The visit

Suitable for any place and circumstance, this position has the flavor of a surprise encounter. Standing, facing each other, the man stimulates with his own sex that of the partner until he reaches a superficial penetration.

To obtain maximum success, it is therefore advisable for the woman to increase her stature by wearing high-heeled shoes or climbing onto any other available support.

Let it Go

The woman is lying on her back on a pillow with her knees bent. The partner is sitting with her legs under her thighs leans forward to kiss her belly, then lifts the pelvis to penetrate. The man begins to move rhythmically when the woman is abandoned.

The butterfly

She stretches out on a fairly tall and comfortable piece of furniture, he stands in front of her and takes the partner's legs leaning them over his shoulders. She lifts her arms up raising her pelvis while he helps her by pushing her butt upwards. By maintaining this position he will be able to move inside her at the perfect angle to orgasm.

The position of the butterfly in practice

While requiring a certain skill, the position of the Butterfly must not be frightening as the two bodies tend to support each other, as long as the right angle is found. First of all, you will have to put yourself on a piece of furniture in which its basin is lower than yours: a table, a desk, the washing machine, the dishwasher ... but it will also depend on how tall you are. The moment you lift your pelvis, your back must form a straight line with its pelvis. In this way, your pubis and his will fit together and he will be able to penetrate you perfectly and without making excessive efforts. To avoid arching your back you will need to ask your partner to support your pelvis with his hands. But you will see that it will be natural for him to do so in order to move more easily.

A stimulating position

If you feel comfortable in this position (maybe because you do yoga every day or because you have good abdominals), you can use one hand to stroke your breast or masturbate. You will see that your partner will become even more excited seeing that you caress yourself under his eyes. A variant of the classic position in which the man lifts his partner's pelvis to improve the angle of penetration, the butterfly position is original not only because the woman is in an unusual position, but above all because it is practiced outside the bed. And this is already enough to break the routine and make the situation more exciting for both.

An exclusive orgasm

The Butterfly position is a position that is worth trying also because it promotes vaginal orgasm. In fact in the Butterfly the penetration is deep but it is not parallel to the vaginal canal, as for example in the Missionary position. In doing so, the stimulated area is not the bottom of the vagina, but the anterior part, therefore the G point. The resulting orgasm is strong and makes all the senses vibrate!To add a note of pleasant sensuality to the situation you can also focus on the details: red flowers, candles, incense sticks, two glasses of champagne, romantic background music. With a little imagination, the play between the bodies will be even more intense and spicy.

The Bracket
The woman is stretched out with her belly up, and her buttocks on the edge of the bed. The man is standing and penetrating her stroking her breasts and clitoris. This position can also be done while standing still. In this case, the woman hugs her partner by crossing her legs. It is very exciting: the woman feels the pulsations of the penis and the man those of the vagina.

Special chair
The woman sits on him giving him his shoulders and using his arms as a support, he penetrates her from behind and helps her move until the pleasure is achieved.

The Mermaid
She has to lie down on a table, a bed, or a desk, placing a pillow under her buttocks which must be slightly raised. Then always the woman must raise her legs up, keeping them together. The woman can put her hands under the pillow to give a little more elevation to the pelvis. He performs the penetration while she has her legs up; if the bed or table is low, the man should bend his knees or kneel on the ground. In addition, he can grab his feet to leverage, so as to be more stable if he wants to push deeper.

Scissors

She is lying supine on a table, with her pelvis at the edge and stretching her legs upwards. The man is standing in front of her and holds her by the ankles penetrating her. In making the move, the man continues to open and close the woman's legs, mimicking scissors.

Let yourself be tempted by the unique sensations of bondage. If you like having sex on your feet this is the position for you! If you don't feel like dominating, let yourself be carried away by the impetus of your him.

The Climb

The man is firmly on his feet and lifts the woman who is standing before him. She wraps it with her legs, keeping her feet on a bed or sofa. The man makes the woman go up and down, trying to produce a movement from top to bottom while maintaining the same speed and depth.

Sexy 5

The woman must sit on a piece of furniture or a table and the man must stand in front of her. His legs must be slightly bent, spaced about 90 cm apart. The woman rests the arms on the man, who instead has his arms around the lower part of her torso. Slowly the woman has to push her left leg up and support her right foot on the man's left shoulder. Do the same thing with the right leg on the man's left shoulder.

The Hanging Woman

The man lifts the woman holding her under the buttocks. The woman wraps her legs around his hips to hold on and rests her feet against the wall to which the man has to lean.

Right in target

What you need are a chair, a lot of agility and a good physical shape. She is astride the back of the chair with her torso bent and her elbows resting on her knees.

He holds her by the hips by modulating the swing of the back and forth to achieve maximum excitement.

The Apple

The man is standing and holding his partner in his arms, supporting her by the buttocks and the back while she wraps him tightly with the legs. The woman can also lean with her back against the wall, so as to have secure support and allow greater penetration. This position has the advantage of being practicable in any place but also has the limitation of being suitable only for a muscular man and of not being able to be maintained for a long time.

Standing up

Standing, skin against skin, she turns her back on him while he, embracing her with passion, brings her to him and penetrates her from behind. To keep her balance better, the woman can lean against the wall or at a table.

Relaxing and Cuddling Positions

The French

In this Kamasutra position, the man and the woman are lying on their sides. Her buttocks adhere to the partner's pelvis which gently penetrates her. A position that recalls the position of the newborn baby in the womb, the French position instinctively inspires affection and sweetness.

The advantages of the French position

The French position has numerous points in its favor: easy to put into practice, it does not require athlete skills for its execution. It is very relaxing and will allow you to have sex even if you are tired and think (especially him!) Of not being able to do it! Before penetration, you can caress your partner's member with your body. Then, during intercourse, he will be able to caress your clitoris and cover you with kisses and caresses.

This particularly comfortable position is also suitable for pregnant women who do not want to give up the pleasure of sex. Last but not least, the French position is recommended for women who want to become mothers, since by promoting deep penetration, it facilitates the rise of spermatozoa to the uterus. The only drawback of this position (if you can say so) is that, by turning your back on your partner, you cannot look him in the eye.

But the contact between the bodies is such that you can still perceive all its vibrations. And then, to add a further note of romance to the atmosphere, you can decorate the bedroom with roses and candles and put a soft light.

The Vertical Hug

The man lies on his stomach, keeping his legs slightly apart. The woman lies on him on his stomach, letting herself be penetrated and stretching her legs until they are completely extended in the middle of his legs. It is an excellent position for constant contact between partners and for shallow penetration.

Simplicity

She is lying on her back with her legs spread as he penetrates her. The hands remain free to exchange caresses and effusions. Especially those of the woman, who can passionately caress the man's back and buttocks. A position to make love in all simplicity.

Front and back

She, lying in a supine position, folds her thighs on her belly and rests her feet on the partner's shoulders. Kneeling on her the man penetrates her deeply. This position can provide enormous pleasure to the woman, especially during ejaculation, provided that the vagina is sufficiently lubricated to prevent the particularly intense penetration from being painful.

The bell

the woman is bent forward and the man penetrates her while sitting semi-seated. Taking hold of her feet, she moves slowly as he covers her back with kisses. It is a position that requires agility but that allows you to rediscover often forgotten corners of your partner's body.

Crisscross

The woman lies down on one side with her arms above her head. The man has to stand perpendicular on the woman's side, and slowly the woman has to lift her left leg and make the man put his lower body between his legs.Once she is well united, the woman must grab the man by the shoulders while anchored on the floor.

Siesta in couple

We suggest this position as a relaxing stop during your "love marathon". You will enjoy a sweet doing nothing made of looks and caresses. Even your body will benefit from the drop in pressure, recommended before resuming more demanding erotic games.

The Laying Char

The man leans on his hands. The partner reclines comfortably on some pillow with her legs resting on the man's shoulders and moves rhythmically. This position allows a deep penetration and causes a very intense pleasure.

Orient secrets

He is straight on his knees while the woman, in a supine position and with her legs bent, rests her feet against his chest. The man can bend backward or forwards, thus moving away or bringing the partner's thighs closer to his breast. This position allows very deep penetration.

Passionate Proposal

The position of the passionate proposal requires a little practice and a lot of will. Kneeling face to face, the man puts his foot firmly planted on the ground in front of him (as if he were making a marriage proposal) and the woman puts her right foot on the ground, climbing over his kneeling leg.

The penetration can be done by leaning forward towards the planted feet, making lunges, as if you were dancing slow.

The pinwheel

The woman and the man are lying facing each other. The woman must bring her groin closer to hers, wrapping her legs around the sides of her torso. Her arms must be extended behind to support the weight. He surrounds the woman's waist with his legs and holds her thighs, gently pushing.

The sandwich

The woman stretches out on the man, spreads her legs apart to facilitate penetration, and immediately closes them so that the two bodies are perfectly superimposed. He then begins to stimulate his partner by rubbing his own body against that of his partner laterally and horizontally. It is a very intimate position that allows maximum physical contact and satisfies minute women who usually prefer to be on top.

The Lazy 2

The man kneels with his buttocks resting on his heels and supports himself with his arms. The woman is lying on the bed with her head on the pillow and her back well stretched out. To allow optimal penetration, raise your partner's tight thighs. It can stimulate other areas by dispensing stroking the breasts and the mount of Venus. Particularly sexy and exciting, this position offers deep penetration and offers partners the opportunity to observe each other.

Bonding

The Lazy Man

The man is lying with his legs dangling at the edges of the bed and his feet on the ground while the woman, resting on him, keeps her thighs wide apart to allow the partner to stimulate her clitoris and she to caress the base of the penis. To increase penetration, she moves rhythmically, gripping her knees. This position offers the man a particularly exciting view of his partner's penetration, buttocks, and sex. Taking advantage of the free hands, it can also stimulate the anal area and the buttocks.

The ascendant

The man and the woman are facing each other on their knees. He tucks his thighs into hers. This particularly intimate position allows the two lovers to embrace, kiss, caress in a swirling interweaving of passion and desire.

The Joint
The man and the woman are lying side by side in a fetal position. The woman sticks her pelvis to that of her partner and crosses her legs. The man caresses the woman's clitoris during intercourse. Before penetration, the woman can caress the member of her partner with her body. This position proves to be very stimulating if accompanied by caresses.

The Confession
The man sneaks gently between the partner's legs. She is lying on her side with her knees bent, her feet crossed and she squeezes him tightly with her legs. During the penetration, he can caress his sex and the back of his neck. Taking advantage of this position made of intimacy and sweetness, the two lovers can share pleasures and desires to be discovered together.

Don't Go
The man is lying on his side. The woman lies down next to him with her head at the height of the feet and squeezes his pelvis with her thighs raised rubbing it with her breasts. Particularly excited from the point of view, during penetration he can caress her buttocks and gently insert his fingers into the anus, a highly erogenous zone.

Zen

This position is ideal for taking a breather between more complex positions that require more "work". The man and the woman are lying on their sides looking at each other and the legs are crossed one to the other to facilitate penetration. The movements must be practically in unison and can be alternated between slow and faster until orgasm is reached.

Woman Dominates Positions

The Spanish

In this position, the man rests one hand on the ground and sits with his legs stretched out while the woman, on her back, kneels astride him and moves rhythmically. In the Spanish position, it is the woman who has an active role, even if in any case the partner can swing the back of her partner and therefore intervene in the rhythm of the penetration, thanks to the hand that is free. Moreover, to make the position even more exciting, the partner can caress her partner's breasts, buttocks, and clitoris while taking advantage of a splendid view of her lower back!

A voluptuous position

Easy to perform position, both for him and for her, the Spanish position guarantees deep penetration and strong sensations for both partners. If you like being on top and amaze your partner, this position is made for you! Of course, you won't have to be afraid to show your B side, and if you think your partner can see your little flaws, know that he won't even notice! If you are a romantic girl and you don't want to be able to look into your eyes Comrade, you could overcome this inconvenience by creating an erotic atmosphere: rose petals, background music, soft lights, a glass of sparkling wine ... each of these details will add a note of sensuality to the situation. Or, simply stand in front of a mirror and look at each other in this unusual way and for this reason even more exciting!

The Spanish position can be considered a variant of the famous position of the doggie. Deep penetration, the possibility of wide and slow movements: the two positions have many advantages in common, with the difference that in the Spanish position the man is sitting on the ground and therefore the woman is in command.

Back View

On the bed, the man is seated and his legs are stretched out horizontally. The woman must creep under her legs in a rear position and help penetration. The woman then has to stretch her legs, trying to put them behind him, and relax her torso between his feet. The woman must then slide up and down using his feet to leverage.

Riding Backwards

The man is lying on his back. The woman is astride him backward. The woman can caress the partner or the clitoris by moistening her fingers with saliva or vaginal secretions.

Sitting face to tits

The man is seated on the ground or on the bed with one elongated leg and the other slightly bent to feel well in balance. The woman reclines on him astride rising and sitting rhythmically while the partner supports her by the buttocks. The man can also stimulate his partner's breasts with kisses and pacifiers or have fun nibbling her nipples.

The Amazon

Mythical position of the Kamasutra, the Amazon is also among the most practiced and appreciated by women. Why? We will explain it to you right away ...

A bit of history...

But first of all, what is the origin of the name of this position? You must know that in ancient times the Amazons were a people of female warriors. Between myth and reality, these women have made a lot of talk about them, provoking numerous erotic fantasies. Vestige of this legend in which women take power over men, in the position of the Amazon the woman becomes the architect of her pleasure and dominates the man by placing herself on him, like a rider on his horse. Practiced since ancient times, the position of the Amazon is also known as the "position of Andromache". In fact, the wife of Hector, the hero of Homer's Iliad, used to practice this position.

The position of the rider in practice

Going to the point, in this position the man is lying on his back with his legs close together. The woman reclines on him and begins to ride him, moving the body according to the movement and inclination that she prefers. To vary the rhythm and depth of the penetration, you can use your feet as support or bring your torso backward using your arms.

A comfortable position for both and easy to practice, in the Amazon you are in charge, while the man, immobilized by your body, is lulled by the rhythmic movements that you perform and has his hands free to stimulate your breast and clitoris.

Intense pleasure for her

If women like Amazon so much, there is a reason, and this is that this position promotes vaginal orgasm. In fact, in order for a position to favor female pleasure, the penis must stimulate the G-spot area, rather than the bottom of the vagina, such as in the missionary position. In the Amazon of the Kamasutra the two partners are facing each other and the penetration is a little bias and deep. The anterior area of the vagina is therefore stressed by movements, making this position particularly conducive to stimulating the G-spot and therefore to the female orgasm. Here is revealed the secret of the Amazon's position!

And for him?

So, all selfish, women who practice or who want to try this Kamasutra position? Not really, as much as the Amazon gives him intense pleasure. Comfortably relaxed, your partner can let go and take full advantage of the sensations brought about by your movements. For him, the vision of your body moving on him will be very stimulating and he will be able to participate in the action by caressing you.

A location for all occasions

Sensual and exciting position for both partners, the Amazon can also be practiced sitting and dressed. In short, when desire makes itself felt, there is always a way to satisfy it thanks to this position!

Another advantage of the Amazon is that being the woman to dictate the rhythm of the movements, male pleasure increases more progressively: it will therefore be a position to be privileged if your him tends to ejaculate quickly.

To vary ...

The position of the Amazon is also practical because it can be performed in many different ways: from lying down, sitting, on a chair, on the bed, on the sofa. Furthermore, if you want to offer your partner the vision of your lower back, you can try the position of the Viking Ride, in which the woman sits astride the partner and gives him her back. The man holds it by the high end of the thighs, modulating if he wishes, the oscillation of the back and forth. And since the eyes also want their part, in this position your man will have a heavenly vision of your B side!

The Sofa

The man is sitting on a sofa or chair, with his back resting. His feet must be resting on the ground. The woman sits on the man, facing him. The woman then moves the upper body downwards, backward, resting it on his thighs, and placing her hands backward, on the floor to keep herself. Then he opens and closes his legs to get into the rhythm.

The English Mount

He lies on his back keeping his legs slightly apart and his head resting on the pillow. She leans on him sideways, with the legs on one side and the rest of the body on the other, keeping his legs well closed and leaning on the arms for better support. At the moment of penetration, she opens her legs slightly and begins to make circular, slow, and continuous movements, alternating with vertical movements. To facilitate orgasm, the man can carry out movements equal and opposite to those of the woman.

The tarantula

The man is resting on his hands, the legs are stretched on the bed. The woman is astride him and rests her hands next to his legs. The woman goes back and forth rhythmically with the pelvis.

Bite her Hairs

The man is lying on his back. She is lying on him resting on her elbows, with semi-flexed legs. The man penetrates the partner holding her for life. The woman lifts her pelvis then leans it against him.

Hot Rubbing

Leaning on one arm, the man is seated on his side and holds one knee on the ground. Leveraging his forearms and giving him his shoulders, the woman rubs on her sex and moves rhythmically to facilitate penetration.With his free hand, he can also caress her breasts, buttocks, and anal area. It is advisable to practice this position on a carpet rather than on the bed.

The Viking ride

The woman leans back to her partner and reclines around him. The man holds her by the high end of the thighs and modulates the oscillation of the back and forth. This position allows the woman to caress the partner's scrotum, while the man can appreciate the partner's buttocks up close.It is an easy position to perform especially for the partner, who is pleasantly seated. It is also a comfortable position for men, as it is relaxed and has a beautiful view!

Furthermore, if you are a girl who does not like positions in which the woman has a passive role, know that this position is made for you as it is not said that the man controls movements, indeed! In fact, if it is the man who modulates the oscillation, it is the woman who guides the penetration, moving the body according to the movement and inclination that it wants. You can place your hands onman's legs and you can tilt yourself back forward or backward, to change the angle of penetration. In short, in this position neither the man nor the woman controls, and the greater the complicity between the partners, the more coordinated the movements and the better the sensations experienced by both.

This position allows the woman to caress the man's genitals and the man, in turn, to caress the woman's back. In fact, if he lets the woman guide the movements, the man will have his hands completely free and he will also be able to appreciate the partner's B side closely!

An exciting position for both

Highly erotic position, we can consider this position as a variant of Amazon's position, as in this case too the woman is sitting astride the partner, albeit from her back. The Viking ride is a position that facilitates vaginal orgasm in how much you can control the penetration and then find the angle that allows you to experience greater pleasure. The clitoris is also stimulated by rubbing, and if you feel comfortable in this position it may also masturbate while you move.

For men, this position is very exciting as it can completely let go and feel the pleasure growing. However, some men do not appreciate this position because subjected to the rhythm of their partner, they do not have total control of their pleasure, and they feel destabilized by this situation.

To feel at ease ...

You too may be reluctant to try this position as you cannot look your partner in the eye, but only perceive his reactions from his moans and movements. Furthermore, knowing that your partner can observe your back and his small defects at will (even if, of course, your partner misses it), you may feel uncomfortable. But the solution exists: why don't you offer your man to blindfold himself? Doing so would better savor your every move! Furthermore, since the position does not allow you to exchange languid looks looking into your eyes, you can enhance the romantic atmosphere by decorating the bedroom with roses and candles, lowering the light, and putting a little background music. To have eye contact with your partner, you can easily alternate this position and the position of the Amazon. In short, the tricks exist to make this position not only very conducive to orgasm but also very sensual!

The Steamer
He is lying on his back. She sits on her sex with her legs on her side and her thighs spread apart and move rhythmically. The woman can increase the pleasure of deep penetration by caressing herself.

Man Dominates Positions
Doggy Style
The woman stands on all fours, holding her arms out in front of her head. To maintain balance, the woman shifts the weight onto her hands, keeping her head down. The man kneels behind the woman, holding her hips. The position, also called doggy style, is one of the classics of the Kama Sutra.

Legs on shoulder

She lies down with a pillow under her head and legs in the air as straight and as high as possible. The man is on his knees in front of her, taking her legs and resting them on one shoulder. Pushing forward, he penetrates her, wanting to use the bed or the floor as support by leaning with the other arm.

Slipping

The woman is lying on her stomach on the bed or on the floor, with her legs stretched out and slightly apart. The man sits behind her and arches his body to facilitate penetration, holding onto his arms and resting his hands on the sides of her legs. To intensify the sensations, the woman may slightly close her legs. For convenience, it is recommended that the woman leaning on her elbows.

The Candle

The woman is lying on her back with her legs vertical. The partner, kneeling on the bed or on the ground, lifts her pelvis and penetrates her caressing the lower part of her thighs, a particularly erogenous zone.

The position of the candle in practice

To be more comfortable, the woman can put a pillow under her head and possibly also under her back, so as not to strain the lower back too much. The position of the Candle is in fact a rather acrobatic position for the woman: it, therefore, requires a good physical shape and therefore well-trained abdominal muscles! If you are not very trained, you can still ask your partner to help you lift your pelvis with his hands. To maintain the position more easily, your partner can tighten your pelvis between his thighs. Of course, if you practice yoga for yourself this position will be a breeze!

An exciting location

The advantage of the position of the Candle is that your partner has his hands free to caress not only your thighs but also your clitoris. But you too, if you feel comfortable in this position, you could masturbate while your partner penetrates, making the game even more exciting, both for you and him because he certainly will not mind watching you while you caress ... Also during the action you can exchange glances and sweet or fiery words.

To add a spicy and sensual note to the situation you can ask your partner to blindfold you. This way you can take advantage of every sensation without worrying about what's going on around you. You can decorate the room with roses and candles or put two glasses of sparkling wine in plain sight on a handy tray ...

The position of the candle is interesting because it allows you to have sex by stimulating new muscles and new parts of the body. The sensations change and the senses awaken, especially if in recent times you have always made love in the same position.

An exceptional experience for fans of clitoral orgasm If you don't want to dominate, let yourself be carried away by the impetus of your him Guaranteed orgasm An excellent position if he has a small penis Pamper your G-spot, you won't regret it!

The Eight

The woman is lying on her back, with her legs slightly open, possibly with a pillow under her back to facilitate penetration. The man is lying on the woman and has his hands on one side and the other of her head, with his arms stretched out as if doing the push-ups. The woman holds her hands on the man's hips and helps him form "8" numbers with the hips while he is inside her. The 8 "relaxed" is the symbol of infinity, and it seems like a good promise to be made in two!

Flexuosity

The woman has her knees bent on her belly while the man, kneeling, penetrates her by leaning on one hand and holding the partner's thighs with the other. By taking advantage of the hands-free, she can caress the base of the penis.

Even if it needs good agility, this position allows deep penetration and favors fertilization.

The Star

The woman is lying on her back, one leg stretched out, the other bent. The man is above her, passes one leg under her raised his thigh, and leans on his elbows. This position is very stimulating: the woman can caress her own body and that of her partner throughout the duration of the intercourse.

Bandoleer

The woman is lying on her back with her legs raised and her knees joined against her chest, the man kneels and penetrates her. In this position, the G-spot is stimulated more intensely.

Samba

The woman is lying on her side on the bed or on the floor, with her legs stretched out at an angle of ninety degrees (L-shaped). He is lying behind her penetrating her as he raises his torso with his arms, placing his hand higher on the opposite side of his body next to his chest and turning around a bit. It is the man who controls all the movement.

Look me in the eye

Here is a variant of the missionary's classic and universally appreciated position. The woman is lying with her thighs apart and a few pillows under her buttocks to optimize the angle of penetration. The man reclines between his legs and leans on his forearms to better modulate the oscillation of back and forth. This position, at the same time stimulating and relaxing, allows the couple to look at each other, kiss, and embrace each other despite limits the freedom of movement of the woman, proving to be sometimes boring.

The Lateral Join

With her back to her partner lies down on her side. The man kneels behind the woman so that the two bodies are perpendicular. The man takes the woman's lower leg and moves it while penetrating her. She takes her upper leg and stretches it slightly to give him better visibility. To get used to the push he can hold the woman by the hips.

The Let's go home

Clinging to your partner, the Let's go home position will make you live a romantic and exciting moment.

In this position the woman is lying on her stomach, even better if with a pillow under the buttocks to slightly raise the pelvis. The woman moves her hips while he penetrates her. It is a perfect location after a romantic dinner because it also helps digestion.

Dirty Dance

She lies down on a rigid surface, like the floor, faces upwards, and bends her knees on her belly, keeping her arms stretched along the surface, above her head.

He stands over her with his legs straight and outstretched and his arms stretched over his partner's shoulders. In this way, he penetrates her and controls the movement with large circular movements or with strong rhythmic pushes, as she likes more.

The Sphinx

The woman leans on her arms with a bent leg. The man above her moves rhythmically.

Adoration

She is crawling, resting comfortably on her elbows. He keeps with his knees bent, embraces her, and penetrates her from behind. This classic position is pleasant for both. In fact, the deep penetration stimulates the vagina and the G-spot a lot and the partner can caress the clitoris and breasts. Very exciting for him, who with this position can satisfy his desire to dominate women. However, some women feel humiliated in this position, while others find it particularly painful.

<u>Nirvana</u>

The woman is lying on her back, with her legs stretched out and her arms above her head. The man is lying on top of her. As the man slides inside the woman, she keeps all the muscles in tension, tightens her legs, and pushes her arms against the bed. This will increase the penetration space and allow a natural stimulation of the clitoris.

Lotus

Lying on her back, the woman crosses her legs on her chest. The man is above her and penetrates her. If desired, a cushion can be used to slightly change the angle of penetration. In order not to weigh too much on the woman, the man can alternate the support of his weight between her legs and his wrists, while the woman can increase the excitement by using her hands to caress her partner.

Indrani

The woman is lying on her back, with her knees against her chest. The man kneels and penetrates her. For deeper penetration, the woman can place her hands on his buttocks and pull him towards her, keeping her feet resting on his chest.

Utphallaka

The man kneels on the bed. The woman lies down on her back, raises her buttocks, and wraps her legs around him.

As the man penetrates her, the woman arches her back, getting help from him, who holds her hands under her back.

The Magical Mountain

First of all, build your mountain of pillows. The woman is kneeling in front of the pillows. The man is kneeling behind her, with his legs outside hers. He lies down with his torso on her and penetrates from behind. Be sure to use fairly firm cushions to create the mountain.

Odalisque

The woman is stretched out with her legs spread and her knees bent. He remains motionless while the man, seated between her thighs, gently lifts her pelvis to penetrate her and kiss her belly. A position loved by those women who willingly give up taking the initiative.

The Gold Triangle

At first glance, the position of the Golden Triangle recalls the classic missionary position: the woman lying down with the man on top. However, the trick of this position is that the man has to crawl and the woman lifts her pelvis towards the penis to get penetrated. He remains in this position while the woman does all the work.

Sitting positions

Lotus

The male sits with his legs crossed while the lady sits on top of him. He rhythms the movement with his hands and caresses the partner's breast with his mouth.

The Magical Ride

The man is sitting comfortably in a chair and the woman is leaning against him. As she moves, he nibbles on her breast.

Rocking horse

In the position of the rocking horse, the woman dominates the partner, holding on tightly to him. A sensual and very exciting position for both of them... The man sits cross-legged, holding his hands on the back. The woman sits on the man, with her face turned towards him, wrapping him with her legs.

The man sits cross-legged, keeping his hands on the back. The woman sits on the man, with her face turned towards him, wrapping him with her legs. The woman can thus decide the rhythm and depth of penetration. To free his arms and caress the woman, the man could lean his back against a wall, thus having his hands free.

The Rocking Chair

Stand astride your man, so that you are face to face. Once it's inside you, wrap your legs around his buttocks and make him do the same. Then you and your man should join your elbows under each other's knees and lift them up to the level of the chest. Then start rocking with forward-backward movements.

The love chair

He is sitting on a chair. The partner, resting on her legs, moves rhythmically, rising and sitting down. The man can stimulate her clitoris while she caresses her breasts.

The Lazy Mermaid

The man is seated. She sits astride him, throws herself back, and rests her head on a pillow. The man moves rhythmically and caresses her breasts. This position requires great agility.

The Limbo

He sits in a rather comfortable chair with a cushion resting under his knees to keep them slightly raised. She sits astride, lowering himself on him and raising his legs on his shoulders. He hugs her to help her move and keep her in balance. Once the man has penetrated her, the woman starts to move pushing her legs towards the back of the chair while he pushes upwards.

The naughty

Sit both on the bed and let yourself be carried away by a particularly pleasant Kamasutra position: the Naughty!

The man is seated on the edge of the bed with his feet on the ground and his back straight. With her back to her, she reclines on her sex and modulates the swing of the back and forth clinging to the partner's hands and legs. He can accompany the movement by lifting her buttocks.

Pressed against each other, the position of the Naughty will allow you to exchange effusions and sweet words. It is a pleasant position for both partners because the angle that the woman's pelvis assumes allows particularly deep penetration. Furthermore, both the man and the woman are in charge of the pushes' rhythm and intensity. And to finish while you move, your partner will be able to caress your clitoris and breasts.

The only drawback of this position, if we can say so, is that the Naughty does not allow to look straight in the eye. But the closeness and the contact between the bodies still allows to exchange heat and sensations, and, for the woman, to feel protected by the body of the partner. So if you have a romantic soul, this position is made for you! And if you really feel frustrated because the eye wants its part and you cannot exchange languid looks with your partner, you can still create a sensual atmosphere by decorating the bedroom with rose petals and candles, putting some background music and burning an incense stick, just like the aristocratic Indian couples would have done, to whom the author of the original Kamasutra addressed with his book about love and eroticism, which later became famous all over the world.

Acrobatic positions

The Y

She lies on the bed belly down making her body protrude, from the pelvis down, beyond the bed, resting her hands on the floor to support the weight. He positions himself above her, his legs between those of her. He penetrates her from behind. The man can also take the woman by the hips and lift her back instead of lying on top of her.

The X

This position is all about control: your man is lying on his back on the bed. Turn around and straddle above him, so that your back is towards him, and then lower yourself onto his erect penis. Extend her legs back towards her shoulders and bring your torso towards the bed, between her legs. With both your legs and your man's legs you will form an X. Then start sliding up and down. To get more thrust use his feet.

The Acrobats

The man is lying on his back with his legs raised and his knees bent and hold the partner resting on his sex by the hips. It is he who moves rhythmically while she caresses the base of the penis, a particularly erogenous zone.

Alternating legs

The woman is resting on her back with one leg on the shoulder of her boyfriend. He penetrates her while on his knees, gripping the ankle of her straight leg in one hand and the knee with the other. By taking advantage of the free hands, the woman can caress her breasts or stimulate the sex of her partner. A variant may be to repeat the same movement with the other leg and so on alternating them.

The boat

Kneeling at the bed's edge, the guy penetrates his companion, who is laying on his back. Holding her by the ankles, she slightly raises her legs apart and moves rhythmically. The penetration is very deep, relaxing for her, and particularly exciting for him, which dominates the situation from above. Depending on the stature of the man, it may be necessary to use a cushion to lift the partner's buttocks.

The Drawbridge

Among the most acrobatic positions of the Kamasutra, there is certainly that of the Drawbridge.

As the name of the position itself says, the man must form a bridge with the body, while the woman leans against him and let herself be penetrated. Pubis versus pubis, it's a great position if you prefer the rotational movements of the pelvis rather than the classic up and down. This position can only be performed if your partner is strong and trained and has no back problems. It is also a position that requires a lot of balance. He may also try to raise and lower the pelvis, but the movement will be limited by your body.

This is a very pleasant position as the penetration is deep and the contact between your pubis is very exciting for the clitoris! While he is moving, you can caress his chest or, by moving one arm backwards, you can gently stimulate the area of the inner thighs, but avoid tickling him, so as not to lose his balance. To be able to relax even more and not have to stay on tiptoe, especially if he is big and you are small, try to wear high heels: in this way maintaining the position will be less tiring, both for you and for him, you will have more stability, and you can focus on your feelings.

To add a spicy and sensual note to this position, you can blindfold yourself, to better savor every movement. Also, in order not to have the feeling of being at a gymnastics course, you can create a romantic atmosphere by decorating the room or bedroom with roses and candles ... If you feel inspired by the position of the drawbridge, know that there is one a female variant, in which it is the woman who stands below and arches her body in such a way as to have her pubis well exposed, while the man penetrates her standing on it, with her legs slightly bent, and avoiding sitting on top of her partner, not to drop it.

Among the positions of the Kamasutra that look like this and that you may want to try is that of the Monkey, in which the man lies down and collects his legs in the chest. Then the woman sits on him and lets her partner put her feet on her back. In this case, it is the woman who guides the movements and the depth of the penetration.

There are many positions in the Kamasutra, and you are spoiled for choice! And the more you try, the more you will want to make them yours by adding detail, a certain way of caressing or moving, particular lingerie, or maybe a sex toy. The variations are infinite, as infinite as the imagination!

The Triumph Arc

Your man is sitting on the bed with his legs stretched out in front of him. Get on your knees above him, lowering yourself on his erect penis. Once you are comfortable, arch your back, but be careful not to strain the lower back. Place your head between your legs on the bed and grab your ankles or feet. At that moment he can bend forward and the fun can begin.

Propeller

In a conventional missionary position, the guy is laying on top of the lady. While above the woman, maintaining the position gives the momentum to make a 360 degree rotation. To help him, the woman must guide him with her body, like the propeller over a helicopter, making sure to lift his legs when they swing overhead.

The Indian Headstand

The woman is resting on her hands, her arms are stretched out. The man is at the edge of the bed and lifts her pelvis, while she rests her legs on the partner's arms. It is a position that requires great agility, a little strength and that cannot last more than a few minutes.

Supernova

The Supernova begins with the classic position with the woman on top of the man, standing on the covers. The man must have his head on the side of the bottom of the bed. She crouches on him with her knees bent and feet well placed on the bed as he penetrates her.

The woman bends backward leaning on her arms and moves until orgasm is reached. When the time comes she throws herself forward towards the man and leaning on her knees, she pushes the man towards the edge of the bed until she protrudes until her shoulders and arms are completely outside the pallet. At this point, the woman moves to the starting position until the pleasure for both is achieved.

The monkey

The man lies down and collects his legs in the chest. The woman sits on him and lets her partner put her feet on her back. For more intense stimulation and to help balance, the partners can support each other by holding their wrists.

Gravity

The woman is resting on her back with her legs drawn up to her sternum. He is kneeling in front of the woman, holding his feet. With just the movement of the hips, the man can penetrate her while controlling the movement and helps to keep her in balance. To increase the pleasure she can put her feet on his chest, holding her hips still further giving him extra control and letting him penetrate even more.

The Head Game

start this game by placing yourself face down, face down. With your hands hold on to the lower back and raise your legs and back, so that it is as perpendicular as possible. At this point, your man kneels in front of you, grabs your ankles, and puts his knees at the height of your shoulders. Then grab his hands and ask him to hold you by the hips. You will both be stronger. Hold her thigh to leverage and get her genitals to enjoy an otherworldly experience.

Pinball

The woman is lying on her stomach. The man is kneeling in front of her, grabs her pelvis, and keeps him at the height of the penis. This position leads to excitement very quickly. For a more comfortable variant, the man is seated on his heels, he draws the partner's pelvis to himself, stroking her clitoris.

The Clamp

This position is decidedly complex and requires good musculature for both, particularly for the woman's arms. The woman lies on her side, rising with her left arm and keeping her calves, feet, and ankles on the mattress. The man supports her by holding her by the pelvis and, lifting her right leg, penetrates her. Despite being very difficult to perform, it is a position that promises deep penetration and explosive orgasm.

The wheelbarrow

In this position, the woman stands before the man, who takes her ankles. The woman folds her legs, bringing her knees close to her chest, and leans her legs against his. The man then penetrates her from behind. An acrobatic position especially for the woman, the wheelbarrow requires a lot of physical endurance and therefore, for both, arms and abdominal muscles well trained! But contrary to appearances, the bulk of the effort is not up to you but him: you will only have to keep your balance, while he, in addition to penetrating you, will also have to support your weight, without letting you fall. A real challenge to gravity!

To make the position more comfortable you can put a pillow under your forehead, which will serve as a support. Or to get tired less try to rest your forearms, and not just your hands. In fact, placing only your hands, you risk not lasting more than two minutes, especially if you are not trained. We also advise you to lift your face often, otherwise, the blood will go to your head and you would risk feeling faint.

But if yoga is your favorite sport, this position will be a breeze for you!

Why should you try the wheelbarrow position (at least once in your life)?

Because, like many of the Kamasutra positions, the wheelbarrow allows you to have sex by stimulating new parts of the body and therefore to experience new sensations, to awaken the senses by putting them into play differently. If, having sex for months (or years) in the Missionary position, your senses are a little bit asleep, try to give them a hit of life by performing the wheelbarrow position, you will see that it works!

The variants to be tempted

The position of the wheelbarrow can have different variations, depending on the position of support or the height where you put your hands or elbows. For example, if the woman has her arms fully stretched. The man lifts her pelvis and the woman fastens her legs behind the partner's back, who supports her with his arms.

To make the wheelbarrow position less acrobatic, you can also rest your elbows on the bed, instead of on the ground. In this way, your body will be almost at the height of your partner's pelvis and you will not have to lift your back vertically.

In short, if you think that the acrobatic positions of the Kamasutra are not for you that you are not a great sportswoman, know that you can always adapt them to your physical condition.

The wheelbarrow (alternative)
The woman is resting on her arms and on one knee. The man is on his knees, holding his partner by the pelvis and her unbent leg leans on his side. It is he who rhythms the movement. This position cannot be maintained throughout the whole intercourse because it would be too tiring for the woman.

Conclusion

I developed this book to share what I've learnt through my travels across the world as well as my love of Indian culture.

I hope this article provided you with what you were looking for, whether it was a new career, some fresh ideas, or topics to discuss with your spouse to better your relationship.

The Kama Sutra isn't just a set of sexual positions, as you've learned; it's a method of addressing a relationship, love, and life in general. Furthermore, the original material spanned over 500 pages, some of which were impossible to decipher and others which were completely out of context for current times. For these reasons, I have not attempted to present an identical replica of the original work to my readers. Instead, I attempted to take the elements that, in my opinion, are most important in current culture, and I combined them with my own comments and thoughts. I hope you like the end product and that I was able to express the Kama Sutra's basic ideas to you.

If there's one thing I wanted to get through to you, it's that there's no right or wrong way to make love.

Two or more individuals are free to attempt everything they desire and hence search out new and fantastic pleasures.

It's crucial to grow love and try new things, especially in relationships that we think are stable and have lasted for a long time. This helps us to keep the spark of passion burning and live a full and happy life.

Printed in Great Britain
by Amazon

24782911R00129